CRITICAL INCIDENTS IN SCHOOL ADMINISTRATION

CRITICAL INCIDENTS IN SCHOOL ADMINISTRATION

A PROBLEMS APPROACH TO EDUCATIONAL MANAGEMENT FOR TEACHERS AND ADMINISTRATORS

BY
ROBERT C. MILLS
ALAN E. QUICK
MICHAEL P. WOLFE

PENDELL
PUBLISHING
COMPANY

International Standard Book Number: 0-87812-140-4
Library of Congress Catalog Card Number: 75-43141

© 1976 by
Pendell Publishing Company
Midland, Michigan

All Rights Reserved
Published 1976
Printed in the United States of America

TABLE OF CONTENTS

CHAPTER ONE: SCHOOL-COMMUNITY RELATIONS ... 1
    Christmas Cheer 2
    The Sting 3
    Middleville Fumbles 6
    Too Much Hair 7
    Gay Lib 9
    "Freebees" for the VIP'S? 10
    45 - 15 or Fight 11
    Censor Calvin 13
    Selected References 17

CHAPTER TWO: FACULTY-STAFF RELATIONS 19
    Ms. Thump and "Swats" 19
    A Generation Gap? 21
    A Broken Promise 23
    "I'll Grieve!" 24
    The Weak-Kneed Boss 25
    Dilemma with a Student Teacher 27
    No Telephones for Teachers 28
    The Dating Game 30
    Caught in the Act 31
    Selected References 32

**CHAPTER THREE: STUDENT RIGHTS
AND RESPONSIBILITIES** 35
    Broken Teeth in the Hall 36
    Innocent Victims 37
    The Shop Class Bullet 38
    Drugs and a Car 39
    Muffled Noises in the Closet 40
    The Hallway Conflict 41
    Tick-Tock in the Locker 42
    Alcohol and Athletics 44
    Knives and Vandalism 45
    Hub Caps in the Auto Shop 46
    Selected References 51

CHAPTER FOUR: COLLECTIVE BARGAINING 53

The Superintendent's Ploy 54
Skin Flint 55
Never Say No 56
The Word 57
Over My Dead Body 58
Don't Cross the Line 59
Color Me Heavy 61
When You Slip - You Fall 63

Selected References 64

CHAPTER FIVE: PUBLIC RELATIONS 67

Diploma Diplomacy 68
The Not So Vanishing Vandal 69
The Last Tattoo 71
A Trip Gone to Pot 73
Thirty Pieces of Silver 74
The Zebra Complex 75
Too Close for Comfort 77
Too Much Too Early 79

Selected References 80

CHAPTER SIX: EXTRA CURRICULAR ACTIVITIES 83

The Ghost Writer 84
Soft Revolution 85
All in the Family 86
The Old Sports Super Boosters 88
Good Intentions - Tough Sentence 89
March Madness 90
Blowing Your Own Horn 91
A Railroad Job 92
Add Out? 93
Too Many Irons 94

Selected References 99

CHAPTER SEVEN: INNOVATION AND CHANGE 101

Fly in the Ointment 102
Bookish Parents 103
Being Different at Einstein High 104
The Boss Blows It 106
A Dangerous Precedent 107

    Blind Flight 108
    Bandwagons and Change 109
    Beware of Jealousy 110
    A Directive from the Superintendent 112
    Female Curmudgeon 113
    Selected References 117

CHAPTER EIGHT: SUPPORT SERVICES 119

    Union Muscle 120
    She Breathed Fire 121
    Object Lesson 122
    A Wet Problem 123
    10% Budget; 90% Bitching 125
    Bossy Flossy 126
    No Business of Hers 127
    CIA in Levenworth 128
    Wasted Motion 129
    Selected References 133

CHAPTER NINE: LEGAL PROBLEMS 135

    The Great Imposter 135
    Love Is a Many Tenured Thing 137
    The Birds and Bees 139
    Confidential Information 139
    Who's the Head Coach 141
    The Blonde Bomb 142
    Here Comes the Judge 143
    Superintendent Sues 144
    A River Happening 145
    Selected References 146

Robert C. Mills received his Ph.D. from Michigan State University in 1970. He is a member of the Department of Educational Administration at Central Michigan University and specializes in secondary school administration and personnel management. Dr. Mills has published numerous articles in education and is highly sought after as a consultant and speaker.

Alan E. Quick received his Ed.D. at the University of Oregon in 1963. He is past Director of Student Teaching at Central Michigan University and is presently Dean of Off Campus Education. Dr. Quick is the author of a textbook concerning the Supervision of Student Teaching and has written numerous articles concerning the teaching profession. He is presently serving as President Elect of the Association of Teacher Educators.

Michael P. Wolfe received his Ed.D. at Arizona State University in 1971. He is a member of the Department of Student Teaching at Central Michigan University and specializes in conducting inservice education workshops for teachers and administrators. Dr. Wolfe has published numerous journal articles in teacher education.

PREFACE

The primary intent of this book is to depict a series of critical incidents in education designed to provide school personnel with an opportunity for direct analysis and to individually and collectively arrive at reasonable solutions. The idea for such a book came as a result of a desire, expressed by many university students, for a practical approach to problems confronting educators.

The case study approach has many advantages. It affords the reader the opportunity to study actual happenings in real-life situations. The approach also offers the reader the opportunity to ponder problems and to select solutions for conflict resolution. Although solutions to the problems are desired, it is doubtful if there is any single approach to a problem because time, place, and personalities pose a host of variables.

An additional advantage of the case study approach is the fact that the selections reflect real problems, based upon actual situations. The real-life happenings can be used in a class setting in a variety of ways. The authors feel that role playing and small group interaction will be natural outgrowths. Also, individual reaction sheets are provided for use by students.

Each chapter concentrates on a particular educational concern. The critical incidents in each chapter are preceded by a brief introduction to the topic which provides the reader with an understanding of its importance in the school setting.

Following the narration of each case study, a series of questions are listed that are designed to stimulate creative thinking and discussion. Also included at the end of each chapter are a list of selected references and a student reaction sheet which enables the reader to respond independently or to consult references concerning the best possible solution to the questions posed.

Each chapter is independently written and the book therefore may be adapted to the interest of the reader. The first chapter deals with the subject of school-community relations and the problems inherent in striving to maintain positive relationships within the school environment. Subsequent chapters present other areas of concern within the school setting.

This book could not have become a reality without the assistance and cooperation of a great number of people. The most important group, undoubtedly, was the number of fellow educators who find themselves on these pages. Actual happenings, actual people, formed the basis for this book. The authors are indebted, as well, to Dr. John C. Hepler, former

Chairman of the English Department at Central Michigan University, who read the manuscript and provided suggestions which improved the text.

Special recognition should also be given to Mr. Gene Church of the Office of Information Services at Central Michigan University who designed the cover and to Mr. William Kesling who supplied the graphics.

If this publication promotes discussion concerning incidents in school life, and makes problems confronting all who work in the schools more understandable, we will have achieved our objective. If this be the case, we should be one step further toward attaining the goal of solving the complex problems which face today's educators. It is to this end that the material is presented.

>	Robert C. Mills
>	Alan F. Quick
>	Michael P. Wolfe
>	Mt. Pleasant, Michigan

INTRODUCTION

During no other period in recent times has the administrator in the schools been so vitally interested in critical incidents in school administration. Nor have problems for the teacher in the community, classroom and building been more germane to their status and welfare.

For educational administrators, sensitivity in the art of the possible becomes a key factor to succesful mangement.

Critical Incidents in School Administration (A Problems Approach to Educational Management for Teachers and Administrators) reflects the common practice of problem-solving ranging from the mysticism of intuition to the more careful pattern of reflective thinking.

There are times when you must necessarily make quick decisions as contrasted with responded or delayed judgments. If the administrator or teacher didn't do this, the time spent in deliberating would often spell disaster. Past practices have indicated that in modern day matters you must act speedily by following standards that have, by previous learning and experience, proved to be sound. If you know the right standards and if the problem can be correctly judged by these standards, you can pronounce decisions automatically.

The new administrator and the new teacher have not had the opportunity for past practices and there also may be times the "act" blinds us to new possibilities.

Another input to problem-solving is "authority," including expert opinion. Knowledge of what others report is valuable as one of the factors related to effective decision-making. Usually, however, it is not the whole story.

Acceptance of the opinion of an "authority" because of the authority himself, rather than because of the evidence or reasons upon which the opinion is based, may be foolhardly.

Perhaps, in your problem-solving you should not accept the opinions of others uncritically.

Traditions have value in the decision-making process. However, even if traditions have proved to be good in the past, you must still determine whether present conditions are largely the same as those of the former time. Traditions had their beginnings!

The emotions that ideas evoke may cause you to approve decisions without examining the facts involved in the situation. These decisions are said to show personal bias or prejudice. If the evidence about the problem is considered at all, it is usually slanted in favor of the position you wish to uphold. Persons whose judgment is warped by strong emotion act in this way. They do not test decisions fairly.

Should personal experience play a significant role in the decision-making process? Sometimes there is a tendency, often an unconscious one, that prompts people to make their reports of experiences bolster their preconceptions. When this occurs your inferences that are presumably rooted in first-hand observations become synonymous with your personal desire, you see what you want to see. It may be that when problems are different and you persist in making stereotyped decisions you obviously will be making inferior decisions.

There! You now have all the advice necessary to "plunge" into the thinking part of *Critical Incidents in School Administration*.

The writers intended, as a major objective, to create situational circumstances by using illustrative case reports to stimulate "thinking" about viable solutions or directions in a given problem-solving situation.

The salient feature of the following presentations is the degree the case studies serve as an indicator for cogent administrators and teachers in operational decisions.

Robert E. Hall
Executive Secretary
Michigan Association of
Secondary School Principals

Chapter 1

School-Community Relations

Since the passage of the Tenth Amendment to the Constitution of the United States, public education has been a partnership between the local community, the state and the federal government. Although the past two decades of the twentieth century witnessed more and more federal involvement, public schools and the means of support for public schools are still primarily the responsibility of the state and local community. Because of this, each local school district throughout the United States maintains a unique identity.

With few exceptions in the United States, communities are able to manifest their own destiny concerning the quality of education locally by electing a board of education, voting on bond issues and millage issues, and by indirectly accepting or rejecting policies developed by administrators and teachers. The community acts as shareholders, and the board of education is accountable to its shareholders as in any big business. The superintendent is responsible to the board of education much as a company president must answer to the board of directors. To maintain the present program or facility or to seek improvements, the superintendent makes recommendations to the board of education which in turn is obligated to seek community support. The local citizens or shareholders must be convinced of the validity of the need and of the value of the request for support. The state and the federal government which also have a stake in the educational operation of a community may be identified as minority shareholders.

If a successful school is to operate, all of the shareholders must cooperate in a partnership devoted to excellence in schools. Much of the burden to develop positive relationships falls upon the local board of education, the superintendent, and all other employees of the school district. The best interests of the student and the educational program always are of paramount importance. The responsibility of promoting the school and its activities falls upon the chief school officer: the superintendent of schools. He must be certain that decisions are based upon structured, systematic, and active participation on the part of the people of the community. His job is to promote sound educational planning and policies and interpret these to the community.

Although successful school-community relations depend greatly upon the volunteers who serve on the board of education, paid employees of the local school district have even a greater obligation. For many centuries, citizens in the community have depended upon school people for moral and scholastic leadership. These concepts, required of those involved in educating youth, date back to the beginning of formal teaching within a social structure. It was true in Puritan New England and is no less true today in thousands of communities throughout the United States. Even if in metropolitan areas educators have a certain degree of anonymity, citizens are no less concerned. It is a truism that, if educators are to be respected leaders within a community, positive school-community relations must be maintained. All public school employees and board members must realize that they are entrusted with the welfare of a community's youth. To fulfill this trust and to promote the welfare of the schools is to have positive school-community relations.

Christmas Cheer

At 8:00 a.m. George Riddle, a happy-go-lucky, popular, first-year teacher, reached for his ninth grade homeroom record book. It was the day before the Christmas holiday and a feeling of festivity was in the air. Because Judson High, a 9-12 grade high school, operated administrative homerooms, the students were noisier than usual as they crowded into the homeroom and into their seats. Mr. Riddle's responsibility was to make administrative announcements and take attendance during the 15 minute homeroom period.

When at 8:15 the twenty-five ninth graders filed out with "Merry Christmas and Happy New Year, Mr. Riddle," John, an earnest quiet boy, approached Mr. Riddle, expressed the Christmas greeting and asked: "Do you drink?" For a few moments, Mr. Riddle was startled and embarrassed. Like most of his colleagues, he attended the "Thank God It's Friday" happy hour at a local pub. All at once he realized that these quiet Friday celebrations had not gone unnoticed in the community.

School-Community Relations

Nonetheless, the "Do you drink?" question from a ninth grader was disturbing.

"Sure, I do," he replied at last.

"Hey, that's great, Mr. Riddle, because I wanted to wish you a happy holiday season and I dropped a bottle off in your car." Then as he left the room, Mr. Riddle shouted, "John, thanks, and a Merry Christmas to you!" When George returned to his desk to meet his first-hour English class, he thought that as soon as possible he had better tell Mr. Ruth, the high school principal, what happened. Accepting a bottle from a student might cause serious problems with certain members of the community. Anyway, as a first year teacher, he was especially vulnerable. At the end of his class, he went to Mr. Ruth and told his story.

DISCUSSION QUESTIONS
1. Should Mr. Riddle return the bottle to John?
2. Would you call John's parents to discuss the "gift" with them?
3. Should the school principal suggest that Mr. Riddle keep the bottle and not mention it?
4. Should the administrator confiscate the bottle and keep it for himself?
5. What other possible solutions might there be?
6. Would the bottle of liquor be different from any other type of gift?
7. What should the school policy be regarding teachers accepting gifts from students or parents?
8. How would you handle the situation if John were an eighteen year old high school senior?

The Sting

Bill Jameson, his wife Betty and four children, had just moved into the conservative community of Eckford, population - 3,000, located in a midwestern state. A Vietnam veteran, he had used the G.I. Bill to pay his way through Central Teachers' College. Betty had worked as a cosmetic representative to help defray the cost of Bill's education. Upon graduation, Bill had anxiously searched for a men's physical education teaching position. The economy was tight, the jobs were extremely scarce. After

Harry's Worthless Store

School-Community Relations

several frustrating and fruitless interviews, Bill was elated to receive an indication of interest from Eckford.

Because the former physical education teacher had retired, Bill's timing was perfect. Superintendent Phillips hired Bill and told him he would enjoy the small rural community.

"Our citizens are interested in education and teachers," Mr. Phillips had said. "You'll have a lot of support in this community. Our board of education members are all prosperous business or professional men. Most are well educated, and they'll be very helpful to you in getting adjusted to the community."

The Jamesons had never had a home of their own. At Central they had lived in a barracks type of quarters called married housing. They were anxious to settle down, and when they located a large rambling older home near Bill's school, they bought their first home and moved in.

Lacking furniture, they borrowed money from the local bank. Since Bill was on the school payroll, the bank cooperated, and the Jamesons set out to buy some much needed furniture. Red Creek, a city of 60,000, lay thirty miles east of Eckford. Bill and his wife believed they might have more options in a bigger place, and they spent the day seeking moderately priced stores. Although the Jamesons liked several items, they decided "to sleep on it" and return the following day with a decision.

Back in Eckford, they noticed a small furniture store and decided to stop in for a look. They were greeted by Mr. Harry Worth, the owner and president of the Eckford Board of Education. The Jamesons explained that they were just looking, and Mr. Worth showed them through the store. Mr. Worth's furniture was of medium quality but somewhat expensive. Not realizing Mr. Worth's position on the school board, Bill mentioned that they liked some furniture they saw in a store in Red Creek. Mr. Worth began to cross-examine Bill.

"Do you live here, Mr. Jameson?" "How long have you lived here?" "So you're the new teacher who bought the old Radcliffe place?" "Did they ever teach you in college that local schools are locally supported and that your pay comes out of my pocket?" "We have a policy with public employees in this town that purchases should be made locally. We support you; you support us merchants. I think I better call Mr. Phillips and reaffirm that unwritten policy — I'm sure you'll be hearing from him."

Bill and his family went home with a feeling of dismay. Certainly Mr. Worth's reasoning had merit, but his furniture was more costly and less well made than that in Red Creek. Bill decided to contact Mr. Phillips, Eckford superintendent, early Monday morning to discuss this school-community relations problem.

Critical Incidents In School Administration

DISCUSSION QUESTIONS

1. Would you reinforce Mr. Worth's claim realizing this was the prevailing belief among merchants and professionals in Eckford?
2. Would you advise Mr. Jameson to continue to shop in Red Creek?
3. How would you work out an agreement whereby everyone would be satisfied?
4. Should teachers be forced to support the merchants in the community in which they teach?
5. Is this a legal policy for a board of education to adopt? Explain.

Middleville Fumbles

Middleville, with a century of tradition for excellence in athletics, had a reputation in the mid-western states as the citadel of high school football. Year after year, college recruiters made Middleville their hometown. Every one of the 7,000 seats in the high school football stadium was filled for every Friday night home game. From the foundry to the pubs to the beauty parlors all the talk was of the Middleville Axemen and their football teams. The teams were legends in the community, and Doc's Barber Shop had the complete story of the town's glorious football history in newspaper clippings on every inch of vacant wall space. Doc was the unofficial historian of Middleville football, and he was "proud of it." Last year the Middleville High School team had completed an undefeated and unscored upon season. Naturally the Axemen were Number One in the state. Spirit was really at its peak. The community was waiting in anticipation for next year.

But, alas, evil times arrived. The steel mills and foundries were laying off workers in droves. With inflation, prices were zooming upward. Voters twice voted overwhelmingly to defeat a millage request. Superintendent Tuxtor realized that activities would have to be cut. Two weeks before the third and final millage election, he let it be known that music, art, physical education and all sports would have to be deleted from the program. That is, unless the millage was passed. Shocked as the community was, times were too bad, and once more the millage issue was defeated.

A citizen's group for the preservation of football was organized, and members came to the school board. The spokesman for the citizen's group assured the school board that the group could raise enough money to have a complete football program. At the same time, he stated it would not be possible to pay the costs of all the school's activities.

At the meeting, Superintendent Tuxtor recommended to the school board that funds must be raised to support all of the activities or none at all. The school board, however, many of whom were Middleville football ghosts of the past, felt football was important to the community. The board agreed to let the "football group" raise money for that cause.

When the plan was announced, the superintendent was overwhelmed by telephone calls. Many complained about the decision, others wanted to form interest groups to preserve the marching band, the concert band, the choir, and other extra curricular activities.

DISCUSSION QUESTIONS

1. Should the superintendent ask the school board to reconsider its decision?
2. Should the superintendent make it clear that the board of education acted on its own and went against his recommendation?
3. Should the superintendent request another millage election?
4. What is the responsibility of the community and the board of education to offer sports programs, art activities, music activities and physical education on an equal basis?
5. How should the superintendent handle the pressure calls?
6. Should the school board operate a complete program until the money runs out and then close down the schools until the people vote additional operational millage?
7. What's the best procedure for informing the public about the possibility of cutting programs due to lack of funds?

Too Much Hair

Marengo, a small, scenic, western mountain city, had a great deal of pride in its student thespian group. The students had performed Shakespeare with distinction and had been invited to participate in a nearby world-renowned Shakespearean festival. Since the group's reputation had spread widely, the thespians were invited to the San Francisco Palace to

Critical Incidents In School Administration

present their latest hit — the musical "Shenandoah." The trip promised to be expensive, and the Marengo Players, as they were called, participated in various money-making activities. They raised enough money to support the students for two days in the big city. Plans included an evening for their own production and a day of sight-seeing winding up with an evening performance of the new rock musical "Hair." Although the school board and administration had authorized the trip, the group's faculty adviser had bought the rock tickets. Most parents were unaware of the plans for the rock musical, and when the children brought home the schedule, a small minority of parents and a group of moralists in the community attacked "Hair" by letters to the *Marengo Evening Recorder,* telephone calls to the group adviser and superintendent, and gossip. Most parents were not upset.

The unhappy superintendent suggested to the principal and the director that the trip be canceled. A number of parents, however, thought "Hair" would be a highly beneficial student experience and encouraged the superintendent to allow the trip.

DISCUSSION QUESTIONS
1. Should the trip be canceled?
2. Should the part of the trip which dealt with seeing the rock musical "Hair" be canceled?
3. Should the director maintain the planned itinerary - leaving it optional as to which student attended the musical?
4. Should the director of the Marengo Players have discussed this with the superintendent or principal prior to making the reservations?
5. Should a public meeting be called to discuss the trip?
6. What precautions would you take in order to avoid this kind of community pressure in the future?

Gay Lib

Ms. Sally Reid was a beginning girl's physical education teacher and a recent graduate of State University. When she arrived in Jonesville, a small, quaint New England coastal village for her first teaching assignment, she was filled with anticipation. During the orientation days for new teachers and during the initial organizational meetings, Ms. Reid learned that her assignment included teaching not only girls' physical education, but a class in sex education.

In the previous spring, a committee of citizens and teachers had recommended to the Jonesville Board of Education that sex education be taught. At first, the topic would be a fourth grade unit. In the ninth grade, it would be a formalized class and an integral part of the physical education curriculum. One day a week, the male physical education teacher would have the boys to teach sex education. He would use resource persons, and printed and visual media. Sally's assignment was similar — only to teach the female students. The contents of the course were not specified and the two teachers were free to develop their own course content in the framework of the general outline developed by the committee.

Sally, together with the male physical education teacher, structured the new course. During that first semester Sally became excited about her unexpected work. Although many of the ninth grade girls evidenced little interest, several developed a growing awareness toward positive sexual attitudes.

The young instructor — rather liberal in her attitudes about sex — tried to be frank, and she discussed aspects of sexual education that the committee probably had not considered. For instance, as an active member of State University's Gay Liberation Group, she believed that affection and sexual relations between members of the same sex were far from unnatural. Quite logically, her course included a unit on homosexuality. While Sally did not advocate homosexuality, she expressed her opinion that there was little wrong with it and that society should accept it. Ms. Reid didn't realize, however, that her teaching about homosexuality was becoming notorious and was the topic of conversation at many a Jonesville dinner table, at various beauty salons, and barber shops. Before long, the school superintendent and principal were overwhelmed by telephone calls from irate and excited parents and citizens alike. The focus: Sally and homosexuality and the implications. The administrators had to act. They had to do something. For a long time, they pondered their course of action.

Critical Incidents In School Administration

> **DISCUSSION QUESTIONS**
> 1. Would you refer the situation to the initial citizen and teacher's committee for further study?
> 2. Should Ms. Reid be informed not to teach anything about homosexuality?
> 3. Should the administrators replace Ms. Reid with a teacher with more conservative sexual attitudes?
> 4. Should the administrators support Ms. Reid in her approach to sex education?
> 5. What policy should a school district institute regarding the teaching of controversial issues in the classroom?
> 6. Should a class in sex education be required or optional for all students?

"Freebees" for the VIP's?

As president of Johnson City's largest carpet firm and president of the Johnson City Board of Education, Mr. Sam Greenberg had drawn a ring around the dates February 15 - 20. At that time, the National Association of School Boards meeting was scheduled at Miami Beach, and Sam, five members of the board, the superintendent, and the business manager of the school district were planning to attend. George Rockbury, another board member, and Sam had even made reservations for their wives to accompany the group. They looked forward to putting mid-winter cold and snow behind them and to spending five days in the warm sun of Florida. Several well-known government officials and educational administrators were to speak, and the group session discussion topics looked timely and interesting. So it was not only the holiday but the program's quality that enticed Sam.

Sam's wife, Jane, also was pleased at the chance to go south for a few days. She did not intend to observe the conference sessions. She wanted to go shopping every day!

Then a week before board departure, the town newspaper, *The Chronicle,* published a number of letters, and the editor wrote an editorial about the Miami trip. All the communications dealt with the wisdom of so many board members going to the conference at a time when money was short, unemployment was rampant, and little money was allocated to teacher travel. Restrictions had even been placed on student field trips, and letter

School-Community Relations

writers claimed these were of more value educationally than the projected Miami Beach tour.

Sam and his colleagues were dismayed. Didn't the board of education members serve countless hours without pay? Wouldn't the value of the conference to participants far outweigh and justify the travel costs? Sam's wife was outraged by the criticism. She wrote a letter to the editor, arguing that attending the conference, at community cost, was a means whereby board members could be repaid for their voluntary work. The school superintendent and Sam, with his fellow board members, were central figures in a community hassle. A correspondent suggested that the superintendent should be ousted and the erring board members be recalled. Another writer implied that the expenses of the two accompanying wives were to be subsidized by the business manager. This, it was asserted, was another example of his "tricky" mathematics and budgeting. Citizens in Johnson City were really "uptight."

DISCUSSION QUESTIONS
1. Should the trip be canceled?
2. Would you attempt to refute all charges justifying the conference participation by board of education members and administrative staff as being educationally sound?
3. What might the board of education have done prior to the trip to hopefully alleviate the community reaction?
4. What should board policy be regarding travel for board members to conferences?

---

45 - 15 or Fight

In 1946, the new Blue Beach High School had been built to accommodate 800 pupils. Now 1,200 young people crowded into its hallways, classrooms, and athletic facilities. The thirty year old building not only was beginning to show the wear and tear of years of service but was shuddering under the impact of overcrowded conditions. Classes already were numbering 40 students, and in the growing community, the enrollment would soon reach 1,600! That was double the number which had been planned for in 1946.

Critical Incidents In School Administration

A conservative school board, two years before, had agreed it was wise to put a bond issue before the public. The money, intended to secure funds to build a new high school, was defeated for two reasons: the school administration and board of education's poor salesmanship and the community's "stinginess." Another factor in the defeat was the negative stance by the arch conservative newspaper editor who also was a member of the board of education. Many citizens reasoned that if the editor and board member opposed the new high school, then the bond issue must be a poor idea and a waste of money.

After the fall of the bond issue, there was a shuffle among board of education members and the administration. The superintendent retired and two board members who resigned were replaced. The new superintendent and the board concluded that something must be done to alleviate the severely overcrowded conditions in the high school.

One of the more literate board members read an article in an educational journal. The piece dealt with the extended school year and proposed a staggered attendance plan for students. At any given time, three or four groups would be attending classes. Each group, however, would attend school 45 consecutive days and have a 15 day vacation. On this schedule, planned for the academic year, 900 students would be in school at the same time as the remaining 300 were on vacation. Other board of education members believed this would solve the overcrowded conditions and liked the idea.

At a board meeting, the superintendent accepted the idea. The 45 - 15 Plan — as it was called — was adopted. An explanation then appeared in the local paper.

Shock waves reverberated through the small community. Although rumors had been circulating concerning the proposal, no one had paid much heed. After all, several alternative plans were being discussed. The 45 - 15 Plan met immediate and vehement objections from organized citizen groups. Many questions were directed to the administration and to the board members.

The "Plan" precipitated a crisis in the community of Blue Beach.

School-Community Relations

> **DISCUSSION QUESTIONS**
> 1. Should a survey of how parents feel concerning the plan be instituted?
> 2. Should open forums be held to air the grievances regarding the 45 - 15 plan?
> 3. Should the plan be instituted despite the opposition because you and the board have studied the matter and feel the plan can be successfully implemented?
> 4. Can you suggest a different procedure for informing the public about a planned stage in the district?
> 5. Should tax-paying citizens of Blue Beach who have no children be allowed to vote on a proposed reorganization when they, as a group, are less affected?

Censor Calvin

Calvin McDermott was an honors graduate in literature from a small private liberal arts college in the east. He accepted a position in Rocky Ledge, a community in a southeastern state. He would teach eleventh grade American Literature. Believing that eleventh grade English students should read various types of American Literature, he prepared a comprehensive reading list for his students. The list included some of the "classics" by such authors as Melville, Twain, Whitman, Hemingway, and Steinbeck. There were also books by lesser known controversial and contemporary authors.

Shortly after his first month of teaching, he had reason to believe he might be in trouble. A quiet, intense, intelligent student, Margaret Sims, stopped after class one day and reported that her parents believed that a number of books on the reading list were obscene and trashy. In fact, her parents had forbidden her to read them. Mr. McDermott shrugged off the criticism and said, "There is enough variety on the list to satisfy everyone's interest — read only what interests you." He believed he had handled the problem well. He felt that this seventeen year old girl was rapidly nearing adulthood and should be able to choose her own reading material.

Two weeks later during the third hour, Mr. McDermott received a note from the principal. He stated the Reverend Mr. McMasters and several parents wanted to meet with him after school to discuss appropriate literature for Rocky Ledge youth.

Critical Incidents In School Administration

Mr. McDermott spent the rest of the day fearful of the meeting. He hoped the session would not develop into a "book-burning — censorship" inquiry. He recalled his words to Margaret Sims. Perhaps he should have been more specific. Maybe he should have said — "Read only the following books on the list. I don't believe your parents will object to these." He would not have been true to himself, though. So, frightened and upset, he awaited the 4:00 p.m. meeting in the library.

When he walked into the library at 4:00 p.m., he was shocked. The principal, the superintendent, the Reverend McMasters and a large number of parents were watching him in silence. He espied Margaret Sims and felt sorry that she was having to be subjected to unpleasantness.

As the meeting progressed, Mr. McDermott realized that the word unpleasant was indeed an understatement. The Reverend McMasters accused him of undermining the morality of youth, advocating the reading of obscene books, and promoting the Black movement. Cal tried to defend *The Catcher in The Rye, The Autobiography of Malcolm X,* and the several Baldwin books as important contributions to American Literature. He said young people who were capable of understanding ideas should have opportunities to learn about the various aspects of American culture.

He could not appease the parents. They attacked him in their narrowness and ignorance. They had no understanding of academic freedom and personal rights. When the meeting ended at 5:30 p.m., the English teacher — distressed and depressed — wondered about his future.

DISCUSSION QUESTIONS

1. Should the administrator suppress the dialogue and totally defend the teacher?
2. Should the administrator ask for a chance to think about the matter and schedule a future meeting?
3. Should the administrator support the parent group and ask that Calvin assign only "appropriate" readings?
4. Should the administrator establish a community committee to establish acceptable literature for the youth of Rocky Ledge?
5. What policy should the school district have regarding appropriate reading materials for students?
6. What role should the principal play during school controversial meetings with parents?

STUDENT REACTION SHEET

INSTRUCTOR _____ STUDENT _____

COURSE _____ DATE _____

CRITICAL INCIDENT _____

REACTION:

_____

_____

_____

_____

_____

_____

_____

_____

_____

_____

_____

_____

_____

_____

REFERENCES CITED

1. _____
2. _____
3. _____
4. _____

SELECTED REFERENCES
SCHOOL — COMMUNITY RELATIONS

Brimm, J.L. "Community Resource File: Improving School - Community Relations," *School and Community,* 61:26, November, 1974.

Burnett, J.H. and J.R. Burnett. "Issues in School - Community Relations in the Present Period," *Association For Supervision and Curriculum Development - Yearbook,* 345-371, 1972.

Dady, M.B. "Improving School-Community Relations," *Journal of Research and Development in Education,* 5:91-94, Winter, 1972.

Driscoll, E.R. and D.R. Goodsell, *School and Community, Indiana School Bulletin,* 33:26-30, December, 1973.

Fagan, D.F. "Community Participation in Decision Making," *Educational Horizon,* 52:10-13, Fall, 1973.

Fusco, Gene C. *Improving Your School Community Relations Program,* Englewood Cliffs, New Jersey, Prentice Hall, Inc., 1967.

Harding, D. "Ten Guaranteed Ways to Destroy Community Support of Your Schools," *American School Board Journal,* 160:47, November 1973.

Jackson, Ronald B. "Schools and Communities: A Necessary Relevance," *The Clearing House,* 44:488-490, April, 1970.

McGivney, J.H. and Moynihan. "School and Community," *Teachers College Record,* 74:209-224, December, 1972.

Norton, Scott M. "School Community Relations - New Issues, New Trends," *The Clearing House,* 44-538-540, May, 1970.

Rosenberg, M. "Community Relations: Approaches Educators Use," *The Clearing House,* 48:50-53, September, 1973.

Sumption, Merle R., and Yvonne Engstron. *School Community Relations - A New Approach,* New York: McGraw Hill Book Company, 1966.

Totten, William F. and Frank J. Manley. *The Community School: Basic Concepts, Functions and Organization,* Salien, Michigan, Allied Educational Council, 1969.

White, A.H. "Let's Stop the Home-School Cold War!", *Education Digest,* 37:12-14, May, 1972.

Zimmerman, Herbert M. "The Community and the Schools: Who Are the Decision-Makers?," *The National Association of Secondary School Principals Bulletin,* 53:169-175, May, 1969.

Chapter 2

Faculty-Staff Relations

The efficient operation of a school system requires the harmonious cooperation of those individuals skilled in providing meaningful activities and educational programs for the students. This group includes administrators, teachers, secretaries, janitors, and the other persons affiliated with the educational environment.

Faculty-staff relations refers to the process of sharing ideas, exchanging opinions, and communicating concepts among personnel in a constructive and positive manner. The basic aim is to promote in a school system an atmosphere of unity and cooperation. The process requires tact, diplomacy, and human understanding.

Lacking these qualities, a staff can become divided and factionalized. Administrators must guard against this division and make efforts to be fair, firm, openminded, and unbiased when they work with school personnel.

This chapter poses a series of critical incidents involving faculty-staff relations. Educational management, an effective faculty-staff relations, is one of the most critical areas in the successful operation of a school system. The critical incidents provided in this chapter will hopefully generate a better understanding of the role of the educator in the total process of faculty-staff relations.

Ms. Thump and "Swats"

Myrtle Thump had taught in the Pine Bluff School District for fifteen years. Except for her years away at college, she had spent all of her life in the local community.

Bill Jackson was named principal of the middle school. He had taught six years and had served for two years as an administrative assistant to an intermediate school principal. Bill approached his new position with enthusiasm and vigor.

In his new job, Bill reviewed policies and regulations regarding middle school operation. He was surprised to learn that teachers were permitted without restriction to administer corporal punishment (paddling). The board had established no policy or procedure in the matter and left the subject up to the individual teacher. Bill also discovered that many teachers administered corporal punishment for a wide variety of reasons. Myrtle Thump, for example, had posted a written room policy. Students were given "swats" for tardiness, not turning in assignments, and gum-chewing.

When Bill remembered recent court decisions regarding due process and Fourteenth Amendment Rights, he thought it wise to establish a corporal punishment policy. Specifically he recommended to the board of education that corporal punishment of students be handled in the office in the presence of an administrator. When Myrtle discovered this recommendation, she was furious. She confronted Bill in his office as quickly as she could get there.

"Mr. Jackson, I have taught in this district for fifteen years, and neither you nor anyone else will tell me when and where I can paddle students."

Mr. Jackson explained, but she was angered beyond reason. She stormed out of his office with the comment, "We got along well before you were here, and we'll get along equally well after you're gone."

DISCUSSION QUESTIONS

1. Was Mr. Jackson justified in recommending a change in the corporal punishment policy at Pine Bluff Middle School?
2. What influence could Myrtle Thump have in the community regarding the acceptance of the new principal?
3. As principal, what action would you take should teachers disregard the revised corporal punishment policy?
4. Do you agree with the use of corporal punishment to control the behavior of middle school pupils?
5. What alternatives would you suggest for the replacement of the use of corporal punishment to control student behavior?

Faculty-Staff Relations

A Generation Gap?

When Patty Platte drove her BMW red coupe into the Hillsboro faculty parking lot, it was clear that she did not reflect the typical schoolma'rm image. A recent college graduate, she had rejected several job offers as a model from a nationally famous magazine. Having prepared to teach later elementary students, she wanted to work with little children and test her instructional skills.

Hillsboro, a small school system, was located in a resort area that served the large metropolitan communities of the state. Most parents made their living by renting cabins, boats, and fishing equipment to visiting tourists and vacationers. The lovely countryside was dotted with lakes, pine forests, and rolling hills. Patty fell in love with Hillsboro after her very first visit to the community.

Henrietta Clamp, who also taught in the Hillsboro Elementary School, was a thirty year veteran in the community. A traditionalist, she was critical of a world that was moving too fast. Women's liberation, pollution, the youth movement, and politics headed her list of examples of rapid change. A spinster, she was "old fashioned" in dress and mores.

When Patty bounced into the teachers' lounge and lighted a cigarette during lunch period, Henrietta Clamp was righteously indignant.

"Didn't they teach you young people how to act and dress like a lady?" the older woman fumed. "No wonder our society is messed up when they allow teachers to smoke cigarettes and wear skirts above the knees."

Shocked by Henrietta's viciousness in public, and flushed with embarrassment Patty valiantly said she would let the principal know about the rudeness of her colleague. She suggested a conference with the principal be arranged. Henrietta was delighted. "It's about time we get this settled. Let's meet with the principal tonight after school." Both teachers left the lounge and returned to their classrooms awaiting the meeting with the principal.

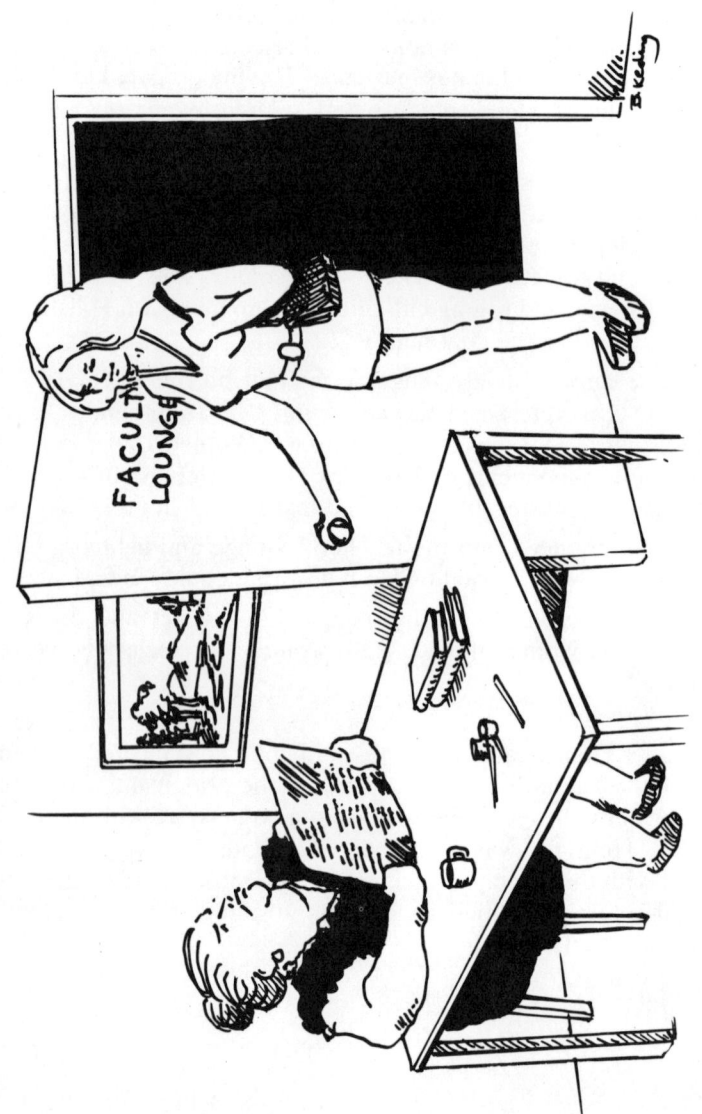

"Didn't they teach you young people how to act and dress like a lady?" the older woman fumed.

Faculty-Staff Relations

DISCUSSION QUESTIONS

1. As principal of the Hillsboro Elementary School how would you resolve the conflict between Henrietta and Patty?
2. Should teachers be allowed to criticize each other in the faculty lounge?
3. Do you feel that teachers should be allowed to smoke and wear short skirts in the school building? Explain your answer.
4. What image should a teacher present to the students and parents in a community?
5. Has Henrietta violated the professional code of ethics by being caustic and critical of Patty in front of the other teachers?

A Broken Promise?

When John English assumed the position as middle school principal in the Carbondale Heights School District, only three weeks remained before school's reopening.

A bright young man, John had been for two years an assistant principal in a junior high school in a neighboring district. He was familiar with the Carbondale Heights School District and was eager to prove his administrative competency.

Unfortunately, central administration offered little or no help to prepare him for his work as middle school principal.

The district encompassed a suburban community of predominantly middle income citizens employed at an auto factory 15 miles away. The fifth through eighth grade middle school enrolled 400 children. The local citizens accepted the idea of a middle school education for their children.

Before he had accepted his new job, Mr. English was promised the right to name his personal secretary. This was a sore spot with Agnes DooLittle, who for three years had held the job. A middle-aged woman, Ms. DooLittle enjoyed working with parents and the school children in the Carbondale Heights District.

On his first day at school, Mr. English got a chilly reception. Ms. DooLittle said in an acid tone, "Welcome to this mess; good luck." This irritated John, but he smiled cordially and greeted the woman. But it soon became clear that something was wrong with Ms. DooLittle. She continued to act "huffy" and replied to his questions with a distinct edge to her voice. After three days of this, he decided to speak to her in private on the subject of inter-office relations. He made every effort to be diplomatic, tactful, and cordial. Her response was sharp. "Quit beating around the bush."

Surprised and shocked, he rose from his desk and walked from the office. "You'll have to excuse me. I have something important to do."

Angered and perturbed, he made a bee-line to the school superintendent. He told of his efforts to be pleasant to Ms. DooLittle and of her sheer ugliness. He demanded that she be transferred. The superintendent told him that Ms. DooLittle had been a good secretary, and the chief administrator was cool to John's request. Finally, he said, "You must solve this problem yourself. We certainly expect your fullest cooperation."

DISCUSSION QUESTIONS

1. What rationale can you think of to justify the superintendent's reaction to Mr. English?
2. Do you support the position taken by Agnes DooLittle?
3. Should a principal have the right to name his personal secretary? Explain your answer.
4. What suggestions do you have for improving principal-secretarial relations in the school system?
5. What is the role of the board of education in the above critical incident?

"I'll Grieve!"

As a fourth year principal of the Lancaster High School, Bob Waters was a positive and dynamic leader. He had maintained staff morale throughout two teacher strikes. As a result, he had community respect for his common sense and good judgment under stress.

One of Bob's teachers was Alex Fernbill, a third-year chemistry teacher, who had received tenure. Alex was a hyperactive young man extremely well liked by the students for his "left wing" approach to politics and unionism. Alex also was a member of the education association's negotiating team. He had progressively become more radical in his views of collective bargaining.

One of the stipulations of the ratified master agreement allowed teachers annually two personal leave days for "professional activities." One week prior to the use of their personal leave days, teachers were required to submit their request in writing.

On Friday morning Bob Waters received a written request for a personal leave day from Alex Fernbill. The day requested was for the following Friday, November 15. It so happened that this was the opening day of deer season, and the principal knew that Alex was an avid hunter who would not miss the opening day of big game season.

So that Alex might clarify the personal leave day request, Bob called him in and requested an explanation of the phrase "professional activity." Alex became very defensive, without offering to explain. Alex thundered, "If you don't give me the leave day, I'll go to grievance based on your capricious denial; then we'll see." Before Bob could reply, Mr. Fernbill slammed the office door and was gone.

DISCUSSION QUESTIONS

1. Was Mr. Waters justified in questioning Alex about the definition of "professional activity?"
2. Do you feel a teacher should be required to justify the use of personal leave days negotiated in the master agreement?
3. On what basis could Alex Fernbill grieve the denial of a request for a personal leave day?
4. Do you feel teachers should be allowed to use personal leave days to go hunting? Explain your answer.
5. What type of a personal leave policy should be written in a master agreement to avoid discriminatory action by an administrator?

The Weak-Kneed Boss

Jack Bellingham was a salesman for the Right-View Audio Visual Corporation. His territory was the midwest area, and he traveled from school district to school district to market his products. He had a reputation for aggressive methods, and was smooth and positive in his salesmanship.

Critical Incidents In School Administration

Over a period of time, he earned the reputation of a "hit and run" operator.

Tom Goodhead's great problem was indecision. He was an experienced secondary school principal of Fowlerville High. One day he discovered that $4,000 of his budget had not been spent for needed audio-visual equipment. Remembering a teacher-survey recommendation, Mr. Goodhead decided to purchase three 16mm projectors on a competitive bid basis.

Three audio-visual companies submitted bids. He decided to buy from the Sight-Line Corporation. This firm's bid was lowest.

About that time Jack Bellingham, in the school parking lot, was preparing his sales pitch — which included reasons why Principal Goodhead should buy from the Right-View Corporation.

When the salesman greeted Mr. Goodhead, the former narrated the advantages of his equipment and volunteered to write up the order.

Mr. Goodhead declared he had decided to purchase the machines from a local competitor.

Mr. Bellingham's eyes flashed. He began a "hard sell," using emotions with direct pressure regarding his product. Poor Mr. Goodhead, who was pretty wishy-washy, signed the order that Bellingham placed before the principal.

When the business manager noted that the lowest bid was not chosen, he phoned Mr. Goodhead. There was an argument, Mr. Goodhead yielded to the pressure. He promised to cancel the order. But when he tried to follow through, Mr. Bellingham convinced the principal to give the order to his company.

DISCUSSION QUESTIONS

1. If you were the business manager, how would you resolve the situation?
2. Should the building principal have the right to order supplies from the company of his choice?
3. Do you feel competitive bids are valuable in choosing equipment for a school system?
4. What suggestions do you have to resolve the conflict between the business manager and the building principal?
5. Should principals spend their time talking to high pressure salespersons?

Faculty-Staff Relations

Dilemma with a Student Teacher

When Jack Miljam was approved to supervise student teachers, he was elated. Having taught biology for six years at Belgin High, he had earned the reputation of being creative, firm and extremely student-oriented.

As the university supervisor arrived to discuss the assignment of student teachers, Jack waited with expectancy. The student teacher would be with him for the fall semester, and Jack wanted to learn about his new responsibilities. The briefing session was valuable and productive. Jack was really excited.

Jack's student teacher was Judy Grove. She was impressed by the organization of her supervising teacher. To her, it seemed hardly possible that within two weeks her student teaching assignment with Mr. Miljam, in biology, would begin.

As Judy gained experience in classroom routine, Mr. Miljam gave her more and more freedom to test her ideas and teaching skills. By the third week, Mr. Miljam turned over to her the total responsibility for teaching the first three periods of the day.

By the fourth week, she was teaching the first four class periods all by herself. The next week, it was clear that Jack was taking advantage of Judy. He was spending the periods in the teachers' lounge. So Judy was handling the entire instructional program in biology.

Sam Dubrow, the building principal, noted Jack's day by day frequency in the lounge and put a memo in Mr. Miljam's mail box asking him to meet in the principal's office for a conference.

As the conference began, Jack said at once: "I know how to supervise student teachers. I do not expect interference from the principal."

DISCUSSION QUESTIONS

1. Do you feel Mr. Miljam was justified in allowing his student teacher to have exclusive reponsibility for the first four classes in biology?
2. What reaction would you take as principal to Mr. Miljam's defensive attitude?
3. Should the student teacher be involved in the conference between the principal and the supervising teacher?
4. What is the role of the university supervisor in the above critical incident?
5. What should be the role of a supervising teacher when the student teacher is teaching?

Critical Incidents In School Administration

No Telephones for Teachers

Since the district's telephone bill had soared, the superintendent in Central Valley School District directed that all long distance telephone calls must be approved by the building principal and recorded on a telephone log sheet.

Jack Allbright, an elementary teacher who was president of the faculty association, violently opposed this requirement. He argued that, if the administration wanted teachers to be professional, teachers should not be required to seek prior approval for telephone calls of a professional nature. The faculty association supported Jack's position. A grievance seemed inevitable.

When Bill Winkle, elementary principal, walked into the school office one day, he observed Mr. Allbright on the telephone. With the call completed, the principal said good morning to Jack as he left the office. Miss Jones, the school secretary, immediately informed the principal that Mr. Allbright had called New York City about textbooks. She reported also that Mr. Allbright had said that the policy of having to get approval for long distance telephone calls was "stupid."

Bill sat down in his office to ponder what he should do.

DISCUSSION QUESTIONS

1. As building principal would you call Jack Allbright into the office for a conference regarding the telephone policy?
2. Was Jack justified in calling New York City in violation of the superintendent's directive regarding telephone calls?
3. Should teachers be allowed to use the telephone to make long distance telephone calls?
4. Can you devise a telephone-use policy that might be implemented in a school system?
5. Should the faculty association be involved in the decision to limit long distance telephone calls by teachers in Central Valley schools?

Jack Allbright felt the telephone policy was "stupid."

Critical Incidents In School Administration

The Dating Game

He was a young bachelor and the assistant principal responsible for discipline and attendance at Mudville Community High School, and his name was John Males.

Mudville was a rural midwest farming community, thirty miles from an industrial city.

Now John was a pleasant lad and a "mod" dresser with a reputation as a "swinger." His ability to communicate and a record of successful high school teaching had led to his new position.

Midway through the school year, staff members at Mudville knew John was dating several high school girls. Despite the fact that his dates were confined to weekends, the "word" spread like wildfire that Mr. Males was attracted to the high school girls.

Several parents wrote letters to the editor of the *Mudville News*. Faculty members openly joked in the teachers' lounge about John's involvement with high school girls.

The staff argued about the appropriateness of Mr. Males' conduct with the students. At last, the superintendent of schools felt he must resolve the situation. He asked Mr. Males to meet with him on a Friday afternoon.

DISCUSSION QUESTIONS

1. Do you feel Mr. Males should be allowed to date high school girls during the weekend? Explain your response.
2. What action would you take as superintendent of schools to resolve the situation?
3. Should the principal of Mudville High School call a staff meeting and openly review the remarks and rumors involving John's dating of high school girls?
4. How do Mr. Males' actions affect his role as disciplinarian at Mudville High School?
5. Should the assistant principal write a letter to the editor of the *Mudville News* explaining John's rights as an adult?

Faculty-Staff Relations

Caught in the Act

When Superintendent George Martino, of the River Valley District Schools, was leaving the football stadium after a victory by the River Valley Panthers, he noticed a light on in the physical education locker room. What had kept him so late was his duty to count gate receipts, lock all gates, and secure all facilities after a ball game. With fans and players long gone, he concluded someone absentmindedly had forgotten to extinguish the lights.

Once in the locker room, he almost fell over Mr. Stevens, the football coach, and Ms. Sharp, the cheerleading sponsor, who were having sexual intercourse. They leaped up, tried to fix their clothing, and stood in blushing silence and guilt.

Mr. Martino shook his head with disgust, turned on his heel, and ordered over his shoulder, "Both of you come to my office on Monday morning."

DISCUSSION QUESTIONS

1. If both teachers are tenured, what action should the superintendent take?
2. How could Mr. Stevens and Ms. Sharp justify their action in the physical education locker room?
3. Does the superintendent have sufficient cause to "fire" both teachers?
4. What action would you take as superintendent of schools, if the woman were an elected member of the board of education?
5. Could the teachers involved sue the superintendent for invasion of privacy?

SELECTED REFERENCES
FACULTY-STAFF RELATIONS

Ambrosic, F. and R.W. Heller. "Secondary School Administrator and Perceived Teacher Participation in the Decision Making Process," *Journal on Experimental Education*, 40:6-13. Summer 1972.

Belasco, J.A. and J.A. Alutto. "Decisional Participation and Teacher Satisfaction," *Educational Administrator*, 40:6-13. Winter 1972.

Brubaker, Dale L. *The Teacher as a Decision Maker*, W.C. Brown Company, 1970.

_____. "Colleague Interaction and Teacher Performance," *Education 95*, 276-279. Spring 1975.

Ellenburg, F.C. "Factors Affecting Teacher Morale: Meaning for Principals," *Educational Digest*, 38:5-8. March 1973.

Heald, James E. and Samuel A. Moore. *The Teacher and Administrative Relationships in School Systems*. New York, NY: The Macmillan Company, 1968.

Howard, A.W. "Junior High and Middle School Teachers' Involvement on the Management Team," *NASSP Bulletin*, 57:110-117. May 1973.

Hoy, W.K. and R. Rees. "Subordinate Loyalty to Immediate Superior: A Neglected Concept in the Study of Educational Administration," *Sociology of Education*, 47:268-286. Spring 1974.

Moeller, Gerald H. and David J. Mahan. *The Faculty Team: School Organization for Results*, Chicago: Science Research Associates, Inc., 1971.

Nathe, F. "Teacher-Administrator Relationships," *School and Community*, 60:21. April 1974.

Norred, R.G. "Relating to Administrators," *Journal of Health, Physical Education and Recreation*, 45:24-25. June 1974.

Olivero, James L. and Edward G. Buffie. *Educational Manpower: From Aides to Differentiated Staff Patterns; Bold New Venture*, Bloomington, In.: Indiana University Press, 1970.

Ryan, D. "Improving Teacher-Principal Relationships," *Education Canada*, 13:25-29. March 1973.

_____. "Teachers and their Principals; Teacher Opinion Poll," N.E.A. Research Division, *Todays Education*, 63:19-Jan. 1974.

Weiss, S. "Program Quality Depends on Principal-Staff Relationship," *Business Education Forum*, 27:42-45. May 1973.

STUDENT REACTION SHEET

INSTRUCTOR _____ STUDENT _____

COURSE _____ DATE _____

CRITICAL INCIDENT _____

REACTION:

REFERENCES CITED

1. _____
2. _____
3. _____
4. _____

Chapter 3

Student Rights and Responsibilities

During the 1970s violence in schools increased from 58 to 117 per cent, and reports indicate that only 1 out of 20 incidents is reported to police. Nationally, vandalism costs the American taxpayers an estimated 600 to 700 million dollars each year. Again and again, parents have ranked lack of discipline as the number one problem in the public schools.

In addition, newspapers report that teachers are injured, raped, or killed while attempting to perform their classroom duties. Parents, students, teachers, and administrators all blame each other for failing to react properly to student control problems. Meanwhile, violence and disruption continue nationally to plague the schools. Solutions are sought to no avail to correct the situation.

Recent supreme court rulings complicate the problem. The courts rule that school officials must implement due process procedures prior to the suspension and expulsion of students alleged to have violated established school policy. Nationwide, state departments of education are requesting school districts to up-date policies regarding student rights and responsibilities to conform with guaranteed constitutional rights afforded both youngsters and adults.

The procedures of due process and prudent judgment require the careful attention of school administrators. An administrator should not approach specific rule or policy infractions with fear or hostility. He must handle each case separately and be sure to isolate with care the issues, deal with the individuals involved, and resolve the problems not only to the best of his ability, but in accordance with due process.

The critical incidents presented in this chapter regard student rights and responsibilities. It is hoped that meaningful dialogue will result from the questions posed and a defensible decision reached by the reader for conflict resolution.

Broken Teeth in the Hall

Sally Hansen, a beautiful girl, was the daughter of the social studies teacher. At age 13, she had the maturity of a high school student.

During the lunch period at the Woldorph Junior High School, part of the student body was expected to spend the half-hour period in the large cafeteria. No one was allowed to leave the building, nor could students roam the building because eighth and ninth grade classes were in session.

One day, Mike Waterman, the principal, was examining a new social studies textbook with view to adoption. Outside the office there was a scream of pain. It was followed by convulsive sobbing and crying. Mike threw down the book and dashed into the reception office.

Sally Hansen, hands over her face, was crying without restraint. The secretary was trying to find out what had happened.

Mr. Waterman put his arm around Sally. "What's wrong?" He gave her a paper tissue to dry her tears and asked, "What happened?" All at once, the trouble was clear. Two of Sally's front teeth had been broken off at her gumline. Her upper lip was puffed. "Good heavens! Did someone hit you?"

She shook her head. Sobbing, she explained she had been fooling around in the hall. When someone tried to "poke" her, she leaped — and hit the wall. Somehow the impact had neatly clipped her teeth. It was her fault, she admitted. No one else was to blame. Several girls confirmed her story.

All the girls were pretty upset by Sally's unfortunate accident. The principal pondered his next move to resolve the situation.

DISCUSSION QUESTIONS

1. How do you diplomatically inform Sally's mother about the accident?
2. Should Sally be disciplined for her "horseplay" in the hall?
3. Is the school district liable for Sally's injury?
4. What procedure would you suggest to prevent similar occurrences of the above incident?
5. Would you inform the superintendent of schools about the accident?

Innocent Victims

Jim Manley, an assistant principal, was maintaining student control in a large, inner city, 1 through 6 elementary school of 1,537 students. The school was located in a socio-economic area where extreme poverty and discipline problems seemed to go hand in hand.

Two students, a brother and sister, were brought to the office for using obscenities in the hallway. They were alleged to have been calling each other names and disrupting classes.

Jim spoke with them about responsible behavior and asked them to explain their side of the story. After listening to their account, Jim reprimanded the students and sent them back to their respective classrooms. He filled in a conduct violation form and filed it in the notebook that logged rule infractions.

The next morning the students' mother confronted Jim and demanded an explanation about his disciplinary action taken against her children. As Jim began to explain, the woman struck him with her purse and fist. It was all Jim and the principal could do to restrain her. She left the building uttering one obscenity after another — about him and the school.

Because of her actions, Jim suspended the two fifth graders and advised their mother that the suspension would be lifted after she came for an interview to discuss the purpose of the children being in school. The little kids wept when Mr. Manly told them they must go home.

Critical Incidents In School Administration

DISCUSSION QUESTIONS
1. Did the assistant principal act in a prudent and judicious manner? Explain your response.
2. Were the rights of the students violated by the action of the assistant principal?
3. What legal recourse did the administrators have against the behavior of the mother?
4. What policy would apply if both students were over the compulsory school attendance age?
5. Can disciplinary action be taken against a student for specific conduct of the parent? Explain.

The Shop Class Bullet

Tom Perkin's father had the reputation of an outdoorsman. The walls of his garage were lined with deer horns, bear heads, goat racks, and stuffed birds. Tom was small for his age. He was the only child of Mary and Fred Perkins, the hunter.

When Jack Tilloson, the eighth grade industrial education teacher arrived at school one day, he was greeted by the janitor who said, "Hi, Jack. Have an exciting day." Jack had little idea that history would record that the greeting would be the understatement of the year.

That same morning, Tom Perkins appeared for the third period shop class. He had a mischievous grin on his face. Several boys surrounded him. Everyone was giggling and smiling.

As the students began their projects, Mr. Tilloson got a call on the intercom telephone to come to the principal's office for a long distance telephone call. Jack said he would come immediately.

Warning the class to be careful, Jack hurried to the main office.

As soon as the teacher was gone, little Tom took out of his pocket a shiny rifle bullet. He had filched it from his dad's gun cabinet.

"What's it for?", one student asked.

"It's a shell. You put it in a gun and pull the trigger."

"That's bosh," said another youngster.

"No, it isn't," Tom was firm.

"How's about proving it, Tommie?"

Student Rights and Responsibilities

Now, Tom did not want to lose face. He wedged the cartridge into a vise, warned the boys to stand back, and brought a hammer to the work bench. Then with all his strength, he whammed the end of the bullet. The explosion was deafening. Somehow, the bullet shattered the glass covering on the clock face upon which was written, "safety first."

Someone yelled, "Mr. Tilloson is coming."

When Jack Tilloson entered the room in the ominous silence, he saw the damaged clock. "What happened?" No one said a word. At last — as if to prove he was a man — Tom Perkins said, "I did it, Mr. Tilloson. I'm sorry. I can explain."

DISCUSSION QUESTIONS

1. What action would you take regarding the conduct of Tom Perkins?
2. Identify the legal implications of a teacher leaving the classroom unattended.
3. Was the principal correct in calling Mr. Tilloson to the office during class time?
4. What liability questions should be considered before reaching a decision regarding Tom Perkins?
5. What disciplinary action should be taken concerning the other students in the class that were involved in "baiting" Tom to fire the bullet in the classroom?

Drugs and a Car

Felix High, a large suburban institution, has an enrollment of 1,690 students. They may drive to school and are expected to park in assigned parking spaces at the north and west end of the building.

Among the duties of assistat principal, Ernie Rayume was checking the parking area to enforce the school ban on students sitting in their cars during school hours.

One morning Ernie looked in a vehicle and saw several "off shaped" pipes on the dashboard. On the seat was a small brown paper bag.

Since reports were common about the students' use of pot, Mr. Rayume decided to track down the driver of this car and examine the contents of the small brown bag. Registration was in the name of Bill Sangal who was called to the office.

"Did you drive to school today, Bill?"

"Sure. Anything wrong with that?"

Mr. Rayume suggested they walk out to the car. At the car, Mr. Rayume asked if the pipes were Bill's.

"No, they belong to friends," said Bill.

"Will you please open the car door," asked Mr. Rayume.

"Sure. But the pot in that bag isn't mine, either. One of the guys that rode to school with me this morning must have left it there."

DISCUSSION QUESTIONS

1. Did Mr. Rayume have a legal right to search Bill's car?
2. What disciplinary action would you take with Bill for the pipes and "pot" found in his car?
3. Should the police be contacted regarding the suspected controlled substance found in Bill's car?
4. Would you take disciplinary action against the other boys that rode to school with Bill? Explain your answer.
5. Should the teachers be informed regarding the apparent violation of school policy by the students?

Muffled Noises in the Closet

John Murphy, a high school principal in Hamptonville, was leisurely checking the building shortly after noon. The assistant principal, Bill Parsons, was supervising the cafeteria and luncheon area during the first lunch shift for juniors and seniors. Sophomores and freshmen, meanwhile, were completing their morning classes and awaited the bell dismissing them for lunch.

In a remote area of the building, Mr. Murphy paused before a large storage closed used for maintenance supplies. Suddenly, he heard muffled sounds. He yanked the door open. Two students were having sexual intercourse. In shame, they turned their heads away. The principal ordered them to dress and come at once to his office.

Student Rights and Responsibilities

In his office, both students denied violating school rules. They asserted they were not in public, nor was anyone harmed by their intimacy. They begged the principal not to notify their parents because they feared physical violence at the hands of their parents.

"My dad will kill me if he finds out," the boy moaned, and the girl began to cry. "My parents will kick me out of the house if they know about this."

Upset and not knowing exactly what to do, John Murphy decided to seek advice before acting.

DISCUSSION QUESTIONS

1. What would you do if both students denied the fact they were having sexual intercourse?
2. Should the students' prior conduct record influence the principal's decision?
3. Have the students broken the law by having sexual intercourse in the privacy of the custodial closet?
4. What are the factors to be considered regarding the possible parental abuse claim made by the students?
5. What procedures would you follow if the male were a tenured teacher and the girl a high school senior 18 years of age?

The Hallway Conflict

That day Jack Sloan walked into his office in good spirits. Principal of the Clancy Middle School, he was in the third week of the semester and everything was operating smoothly. As he poured a cup of coffee, the secretary observed: "We've never got off to such a wonderful start; perhaps it's the lull before a storm."

Smiling in reply, Jack Sloan had no comprehension of the truth of her words about a "lull."

At 10:42 a.m., there was a disturbance in the hall. Mr. Alwart, a teacher, brought a girl to the office. Her left arm and hand were bleeding. Mr. Alwart was pale and angry.

"What happened?" asked Jack.

"Mr. Alwart pushed me through the door," the girl answered.

"That's not true." Mr. Alwart spoke with firmness.

Critical Incidents In School Administration

Jack led the girl to the first aid station and asked Mr. Alwart to stay at the office. As Jack came down the hall about thirty students encircled him. They, too, were angry. They thought Mr. Alwart's room policies were terrible. They announced they would not go back to his class unless changes were made. Mr. Sloan promised action. When he told them they could go to the lunchroom, they thanked him and walked quietly to the cafeteria.

Back at the office Jack asked Mr. Alwart to explain the accident.

"The students are animals, Mr. Sloan. Just animals. They must be disciplined. The girl was trying to run from the room. I tried to stop her. When she eluded my grasp, she shoved her hand through the door window and cut herself. I did not push her, no matter what she says. Then all the students walked out of the room. They think I'm not fair." He paused and added angrily: "I'll tell you what I think. These kids have gone too far, and I demand you suspend them at once."

After Mr. Alwart left, Jack sat down to think. He too was no longer in good spirits!

DISCUSSION QUESTIONS

1. What action should Jack Sloan take against the students that walked out of the class in protest of the room policies?
2. Should Mr. Alwart be reprimanded for his actions that resulted in the girl receiving severe arm and hand cuts?
3. What procedures would you follow to obtain order in Mr. Alwart's classroom?
4. Were the students justified in walking out of the classroom? Explain your answer.
5. Were the rights of the girl violated by Mr. Alwart's actions?

Tick-Tock in the Locker

Bill Fillip was leaving his science class to have a cup of coffee in the teachers' lounge. While passing a row of lockers in the junior high school, he heard a ticking sound coming from a locker. Bill hurried to the principal's office to report the matter and to tell the locker number to the principal.

Student Rights and Responsibilities

But as he entered the administration office, an explosion boomed from the locker area. When he and the principal rounded the corner toward the locker area, smoke and rubble lay in front of the locker which had been completely destroyed. Three adjacent lockers were badly bent. No student was injured by the explosion.

After dispelling the excited students who crowded around the damaged lockers, the principal checked out the name of the student from whose locker had come the ticking sound. The record indicated that a boy named Jim Doyle was assigned to the locker. The principal went instantly to the scheduled classroom to summon Jim to his office.

During the questioning, Jim admitted placing a small pipe bomb in his locker, but he denied any intentions of damaging school property or endangering the lives of students or school personnel.

Jim's record was clear of disciplinary referral. Nor had he ever been in trouble. Instead, he was president of the National Honor Society and a chairperson of the student government. His father, a local dentist, was the president of the board of education.

Jim said he had put the bomb in the locker before taking it to his science teacher so he might see the basic make-up of an explosive device. Jim hoped to enter the bomb at the state science fair, scheduled the following month.

"Gee," he said, "I thought the bomb was harmless, and I didn't connect the wiring mechanism. I don't understand how it went off."

DISCUSSION QUESTIONS

1. As the principal, what disciplinary action would you take against Jim Doyle?
2. What factors should be considered before making a decision regarding the destruction caused by the bomb?
3. Where the rights of other students violated by the actions of Jim Doyle?
4. How would you inform Jim's parents about the incident?
5. What procedures would you implement to avoid a future occurrence of the situation outlined above?

Critical Incidents In School Administration

Alcohol and Athletics

Jayson High's football team had the reputation for being hard-nosed and extremely competitive, and the team was undefeated over three consecutive years.

Jayson was a small farming community of about 4,000 citizens. The district encompassed about 150 square miles, with over 95 per cent of the students being bused to school. Football, in this town, was a way of life. Everyone turned out for the Friday night game at home or away. The fans whooped it up in support of their gridiron heroes.

The quarterback, a senior named Dick Kolaka, had played in every game from his freshman year. He was a true leader and spark plug on the field. Numerous college scouts had seen him play, and he was a hot prospect for college ball. Having been offered several scholarships, he tried to decide which to choose.

The Jayson Warriors' coach — Boots Cooke — had earned an envious reputation in his years at the high school. His 75-12 record and three successive state championships made him a celebrity not only in Jayson but in state athletic circles. One Thursday night after a meeting with the coaches, Boots and two assistants drove to Sparta for a beer. Sparta was a small German settlement about twelve miles away.

When Boots entered the Old Heidelberg Inn, he saw at once some Jayson High School students. There, too, was Dick Kolaka who obviously had been drinking and now was pretty loud and objectionable.

"Hello, coach, you old S.O.B.!" "How's about a drink?" Dick slurred.

Boots turned and left the tavern with his assistant coaches. In the car, on the way home, he said, "What do I do now? You know my policy on players drinking while in training. Here we are on the way to another perfect season and Dick — he's got a future. But he busted the rules. What do you think?"

Student Rights and Responsibilities

DISCUSSION QUESTIONS

1. If Dick Kolaka is of the legal drinking age, is he violating school policy by using alcohol in the neighboring community on his own time? Explain your answer.
2. Should Boots Cooke take disciplinary action against the star quarterback?
3. What student rights must be considered in reaching a decision regarding Dick Kolaka?
4. Do you feel the coach should forget the incident and not say anything about what he observed? Explain your answer.
5. What affect will the coaches' decision have on the other football players?

Knives and Vandalism

As a conscientious administrator, Harlan Dill decided to "catch up" on work in his office on a Sunday afternoon. A series of scheduling problems required immediate attention, and Harlan wanted to be prepared for the Monday morning staff meeting.

When he completed his work, he decided to check the building before going home. Passing the auditorium, he heard laughter and shouts coming from the balcony. He quietly climbed the stairs to the upper level of the auditorium. From the door, he spied two students cutting the upholstery on the seats. He shouted, "Hold it, you guys."

Dropping their knives, the boys froze. He walked over to them and saw the knife slits in chair after chair. The boys said, "We weren't doing nothing wrong."

"Come on, fellows," Mr. Dill replied. "You were destroying school property. Why?"

After a few minutes, the boys admitted the vandalism and blamed it on the class play adviser who they said had not selected them as members of the cast. "Mr. Thespi just wasn't fair," one boy volunteered. "Yeah, he's a phoney," said the other.

Mr. Dill took the boys to his office and called their parents. "I'm suspending them for ten days, and they'll have to pay for the damages in the auditorium."

The parents became angry, and both fathers expressed indignation. Their attitude was, "We'll see about this."

When Mr. Dill checked student records, he learned that the boys were model students with no previously documented violation of school rules.

DISCUSSION QUESTIONS

1. Did Mr. Dill violate the rights of the students by the immediate ten day suspension?
2. Were the students legally responsible for the damage done to the seats of the school auditorium?
3. What rules, regarding school conduct, were violated by the boys?
4. What action should Mr. Dill have taken if the boys had denied cutting the upholstery on the seats of the auditorium?
5. What policy should the board of education establish to improve building security?

Hub Caps in the Auto Shop

Bob Fitch locked the door to the Westley High School auto shop and started home to spend a quiet weekend with his family. He lived in a small rural community six miles from the town. In fifteen minutes, Bob turned into his driveway with the thought of a restful evening with his wife and children.

Westley High was the location of the county vocational education program. Three school districts supplied students to the auto shop program on a cooperative basis, and students frequently used their own cars as "models" for experimentation. The auto shop regularly did minor repair work for community citizens. This not only contributed to excellent community relations but afforded those students, without cars, an opportunity to gain practical experience in automobile repair.

Jim Lynch, a junior, had a reputation as being an honest and efficient mechanic. His forte was tuning engines, and often the highlight of a repair job was Jim's "touch" to the motor.

No sooner had Bob Fitch sat down at home when the phone rang.

"Mr. Fitch, this is Sheriff Johnson. Sorry to bother you, but could you please come down to the auto shop?"

"Is something wrong, Sheriff?"

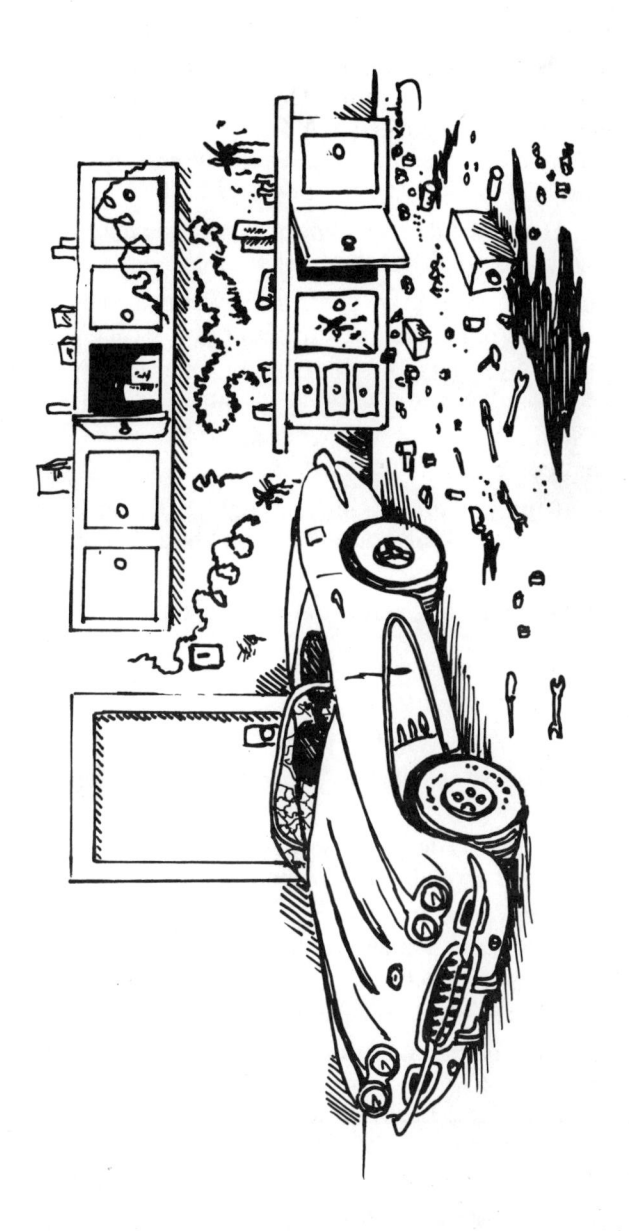

In the shop, tools and equipment looked as if a cyclone had struck.

Critical Incidents In School Administration

"I'll explain when I see you. I'd appreciate your coming right away."

When Bob reached the auto shop, the sheriff announced, "Someone's broken into the auto shop."

In the shop, tools and equipment looked as if a cyclone had struck. The walls were covered with spray paint. The hoist, the tool shed, and the special machinery were "decorated." A Corvette's windshield was shattered. One of its hubcaps was missing. The antennas on two other cars were snapped off. Oil lay all over the floor.

Bob was sick. He filed a damage report. Over the weekend he tried to figure out the why and who of the vandalism.

Monday morning in the parking lot, he saw Jim Lynch and several other boys grouped around the open trunk of Jim's car. When the students saw the instructor, they looked apprehensive; so he walked over to them. There, in plain sight in the trunk of Jim's car was a hub cap, a Corvette hub cap!

"Where'd that come from?" Bob asked.

"I bought it at the racetrack Saturday night," Jim answered. "You know, I guess we ought to have a talk," Bob said. "Come on into the office."

Jim slammed the trunk shut, glared at the other boys, and followed Mr. Fitch.

DISCUSSION QUESTIONS

1. What type of questions should Mr. Fitch ask Jim regarding the hub cap?
2. Should the sheriff's department be contacted concerning the missing hub cap? Explain your response.
3. What procedures would you use to notify the superintendent of schools regarding the damage to the auto shop?
4. Could Jim be suspended from school for the possession of the stolen hub cap? Explain your position.
5. What action should be taken concerning the boys that were talking to Jim Lynch?

STUDENT REACTION SHEET

INSTRUCTOR _____   STUDENT _____

COURSE _____   DATE _____

CRITICAL INCIDENT _____

REACTION:

_____
_____
_____
_____
_____
_____
_____
_____
_____
_____
_____
_____
_____
_____
_____

REFERENCES CITED

1. _____
2. _____
3. _____
4. _____

SELECTED REFERENCES
STUDENT RIGHTS AND RESPONSIBILITIES

Campbell, James, Alexander and Kern. *Constitutional Rights of Students.* Tallahassee, Fl.: Florida Department of Education, 1969.

Chambers, M.M. "Recognition of Civil Rights of Students," *Intellect,* 103:34-36, October 1974.

Edwards, Newton. *The Courts and the Public Schools,* Chicago, Ill.: The University of Chicago Press, 1971.

Greenberg, D. "Children as People: The Underlying Basis of Civil Rights for Minors," *Journal of Education,* 156:212-214. August 1974.

Herbold, P.E. "Freedom of Expression: The Schools and the Burger Court," *Peabody Journal of Education,* 51:124-131. January 1974.

Herman, J.J. "Student Rights: A Program that Works," *Clearing House,* 48:54-58, Spring 1973.

Hoyt, W.L. "Student Rights and Responsibilities: A Point of View," *Journal of Education,* 156:15-20. August 1974.

Leslie, D.D. "Some Implied Legal Restraints on Student Power," *NASPA Journal,* 11:59-64. October 1973.

Mallios, H.C. "Emerging Law of Due Process for Public School Students," *High School Journal,* 57:83-90. November 1973.

Mathews, J. "Legal Breakthrough on Student Rights," *Compact,* 9:18-20. April 1975.

Martin, D.V. "Rights and Liberties of Students," *High School Journal,* 57:24-38. October 1973.

_____. "Position Statement on Student Rights and Responsibilities." National Council for the Social Studies Academic Freedom Committee; *Social Education,* 39:241-245. April 1975.

Sipple, P.W. "Another Look at Student Freedom," *Intellect,* 102: 29-31. October 1973.

_____. "Student Wrongs Versus Student Rights," *National Schools and Colleges,* 2:31-38. April 1975.

Walker, B. "Student Rights and Responsibilities," *Contemporary Education.* 44:100-103. November 1973.

Chapter 4

Collective Bargaining

Collective bargaining is both boon and bane to education. It has promoted partnership in the educational enterprise. Today, at all levels, educators are involved in the decision making process. Teachers, bus drivers, custodians, cafeteria workers, secretarial staff, and paraprofessionals share in actions affecting their interests.

It is an unquestioned fact that collective bargaining has improved communication. Administrators and employees of school districts now discuss issues which in the past never were open to dialogue. For the most part, collective bargaining assures school employees at all levels a genuine hearing about working conditions, wages and benefits.

No one can deny either that the process has improved salaries, benefits, and working conditions for school employees. Without collective bargaining, it is dubious that these advantages could have been obtained as rapidly as they have been.

Unfortunately, there is another side to the coin. "Old Line" administrators have been unwilling to consult others in decision making. Some administrators resent the fact that other school employees not only desire, but demand a voice in decision making. A genuine adversarial relationship often develops.

From time to time, unions have made unreasonable demands upon boards of education and administrators. With money tight, union demands have exceeded the capabilities of many a district. Strikes, agency shops, teacher dismissals or "pink slips," employment of substitutes to replace striking teachers, unfair labor practices, mediation, fact finding, delayed opening of schools and countless hours at the bargaining table have brought major problems to the schools. Between the administration and the other district employees and between the schools and the community, sharp divisions have developed. In many communities, people resent the constant turmoil that accompanies collective bargaining. Corrective legislation has been proposed repeatedly. One truth is clear: Groups must reconcile differences and keep in mind that the education of youth is of the utmost importance.

The Superintendent's Ploy

William H. Finch was the new superintendent of a large urban school district in the east. He considered his election a real "promotion" from his former superintendency at a smaller midwestern district and he knew he had been hired, in part, because of his reputation as an administrator who could deal successfully with fiscal problems. Porter's Mills was a troubled district. Both a millage and bond issue had been defeated — not once but several times. Too, the labor-oriented teachers' groups demanded more and more money. The result was an inadequate school budget.

Not long after the new job began, Superintendent Finch realized that drastic action must be taken. He made a drastic suggestion to the school board: close the schools until the millage issue could be passed. He reasoned that parents, townspeople, and the state legislators would recognize the school district's plight and help.

The board of education would not heed the proposal. The board president said, "Closing the schools would be a terrible political move. Parents would be angry, and the whole city would be up in arms. We just cannot do that."

The next day the teachers union, through its chief negotiator, Red Stuble, presented a list of new demands to Superintendent Finch: an 8 per cent salary increase, small classes, and no extra responsibilities.

The superintendent suddenly saw a course of action which would close the schools. He decided not to try to negotiate a new contract. Instead, he would present certain board demands to the union, who he felt would not meet them. Hence, the union would strike, the schools would close, and the teachers would be blamed. When the superintendent told the board, the members accepted with quiet delight.

These were the board's demands:

    1. A five year contract with no openers.

    2. No salary increases.

3. A longer school day by one hour.
4. A longer school year by one month.
5. The principal would establish all rules and procedures within a building.

DISCUSSION QUESTIONS
1. What do you think of Superintendent Finch's tactics?
2. Do you believe they were successful?
3. How else might the financial plight of the Porter's Mills District be solved?
4. What do you think were the long-range effects of the tactics?
5. How might you have solved the problem?

Skin Flint

Flint, a large industrial southern community, was supported chiefly by a large iron mill located on the east end of the city. It was operated by Jason S. Strong. The industry did not have a union, and Mr. Strong was a benevolent dictator. Although the workers had tried to unionize, Strong had anticipated each move and had squelched it by token pay increases and minimal fringe benefits. Hence, Strong and the iron mill operated year after year with a wide margin of profit.

One day Jason Strong announced his candidacy for the school board. The townspeople were pleased, for here was a man who not only understood fiscal responsibility but would combat union militancy and financial demands of teachers. Upon being elected, he was elected at once the board president. With his labor background and experience at the mill, he was named the board's chief negotiator.

No question about it: he met his obligation admirably. Until there was a deadlock on one issue — hospitalization. The teachers argued for a five dollar a month increase toward their hospitalization fringe. Strong objected on the grounds that the cost would be $33,000.00 because the board of education would have to cover also the administration. In addition, Strong pointed out that the mill workers' hospitalization plan was identical to that which presently covered the teachers. Above all, Strong argued, the school district simply did not have available money to pay the extra amount. An impasse developed. The teachers' organization would not yield, nor would Jason Strong. As a result, for the first time in the history of Flint, the teachers refused to report to work in September. Strong and the Flint Board of Education filed a court injunction to force the teachers to return to work. Later, however, in court, an amount of $250,000.00, for contingencies, was found in the budget. It could have been used to avoid the impasse!

DISCUSSION QUESTIONS

1. What do you believe happened as a result of the disclosure of "hidden" money?
2. What should the superintendent of schools' position have been?
3. Would Strong's actions have been typical of a negotiator for a board of education?
4. Which of Strong's arguments against increasing the hospitalization plan for the teachers were the strongest?
5. Define the role of the board of education and its designated negotiator in collective bargaining.
6. Should a board of education use a court injunction to force a striking teachers' group back to work?

Never Say No

Billy Sullivan Young came to Polaski as principal of the high school with a fine reputation as an assistant principal in a nearby school district. Relatively young, he had the necessary enthusiasm and drive to more than compensate for his youthfulness. Like most administrators in a new position, he had great expectations and a number of innovations to put into effect.

Polaski was a unique community. It was composed of a large ethnic majority and was an extremely tightly-knit community. Newcomers were not readily accepted, and most teachers were locals with years of experience in the school district. One of the long-time teachers was the band director, Sam Jankowski, with forty years of service. He was a great favorite of the board of education and the townspeople.

One morning, in the teachers' lounge during the first period, Sam was planning the band's activities for the Friday night football game. About the same time, the young principal, Billy Young, ran into an emergency.

Collective Bargaining

Mr. Szmarek, the shop teacher, was ill, and no substitute was available. Billy thought he might cover the shop classes by using teachers during their preparation period.

In the lounge, Bill explained the situation to Jankowski and asked for his help. The band director claimed he had a great deal to do and needed the time to prepare band formations for Friday night's half-time show.

"But, gee, Sam, I really need you. We've got to meet that class."

Mr. Jankowski drew himself erect. "Look, damn it. I can't, and I won't. You meet it yourself. My contract with the school district doesn't provide for this. You push it and I'll file an unfair labor practice grievance."

As the embarrassed Billy Sullivan Young left the teachers' lounge, the teachers in the room snickered and laughed. Bill was pretty mad. He hurried to the superintendent's office.

DISCUSSION QUESTIONS

1. What would you do if you were Billy Young?
2. How could the situation have been handled differently?
3. If confronted by Billy, as a superintendent, how would you resolve the situation?
4. Was Jankowski right or wrong?
5. Should a school develop written policies covering this kind of situation?

The Word

Bill Fancher's best friend, George Fox, was suspended without pay for five days. His crime: refusing to turn lesson plans in to the principal's office by Friday at 4:00 p.m. The purpose of the lesson plans was to provide a guide for a substitute teacher if one were needed in the next week. Fox had reasoned that the guide would be of little value to a substitute teacher because it was only an outline. In addition, his history class operated in a flexible manner and was seldom "on schedule."

Now George Fox happened to have a large student following. In fact, he was one of the most popular faculty members of George Washington High. When Bill Fancher's English class for the 6th hour met, Bill knew something was up. The young people wanted to know how long the test would take. He told them 28 minutes. When they had finished the test, students were free to leave.

From the classroom window, Bill saw students hurrying to the mall in front of the school. In progress was a student protest against the suspension of George Fox.

Thad Todd, the superintendent and Jim Hunter, the principal, also watched the demonstration from their offices. Thad had requested Jim to make a list of student protesters and to question them the first thing Monday morning.

That day, Mr. Hunter interviewed all of the students on his list and suspended each one for five days.

Upon hearing of the latest news, Bill Fancher wrote an open letter to the community. In it, he defended George Fox and the suspended students. He entitled his letter "The Word" and distributed 5,000 copies. They were distributed to all of the teachers, professional offices, barber shops, beauty parlors, bars, and downtown stores. Students distributed "The Word" door to door and handed them out to adults on the downtown streets. The school board immediately suspended him.

DISCUSSION QUESTIONS
1. Do you believe Bill Fancher was right in developing "The Word?"
2. Do you believe the superintendent and principal acted appropriately?
3. Was Mr. Fox's suspension reasonable?
4. What would you do as superintendent to combat "The Word?"
5. Was the action taken by the school board fair to Mr. Fancher?
6. What should school policy be concerning student demonstrators?
7. What role do you believe the union will have in this incident?

Over My Dead Body

Myron Preacher was deeply involved in the Ransmore School District. He had been on the board of education for twelve years and, in addition, drove a school bus on a regular bus route for the board. A retired farmer, he admitted the bus job was "Just to keep busy." No one questioned a possible conflict of interest between his two school activities. But when

Collective Bargaining

the other bus drivers organized and began collective bargaining, Myron faced a problem.

One evening at a school bus driver meeting, two of the younger bus drivers advocated with great force an increase in the drivers' wages. Other bus drivers chorused unanimous support — except Myron! He sat in silence, a bit grim-lipped and as observant as a detective. At home, later, he told his wife all about the meeting and concluded his summary with "I'll be damned if those drivers will get another penny. If they do, it'll be over my dead body!"

His wife nodded in agreement. His position thus reinforced, he spoke in opposition to the raise at the next meeting of the board.

DISCUSSION QUESTIONS
1. Identify the implications of Myron Preacher's position.
2. As the school superintendent, what position would you take to resolve the conflict?
3. What do you believe will be the reaction of the community?
4. Has the board of education allowed a conflict of interest situation to develop by employing Myron Preacher as a bus driver?
5. What is the state law regarding a board member's conflict of interest?

Don't Cross the Line

Oil Rapids experienced violence on the evening of January 12, 1973. The western community in the Cascade foothills saw the climax of a long, drawn out, heated battle between the community's teachers and the board of education. On January 12, several teachers were severely injured while picketing.

The story of Oil Rapids is a common one, but the tragic events of January 12, 1973, were uncommon. At the opening of school in 1972-73, the teachers had been unable to secure a contract through collective bargaining. They threatened to strike after Christmas unless a settlement was reached prior to January 2. Board of education members decided to call the teachers' bluff; negotiations broke down. On January 2, the day schools should have reopened, teachers did not report to work. Realizing that their ploy had failed, the Oil Rapids Board of Education resumed negotiations on January 5. Teachers began to picket the administration building.

As day after day passed, tensions built. The teachers, considering that the board was using delaying tactics and was failing to negotiate in good faith, staged a "lock in" on the evening of January 10. The teachers delivered food to the negotiators on both teams and demanded that settlement be reached. In fact, they insisted on 'round the clock bargaining until agreement was concluded. Caught in the turmoil were Superintendent of Schools Roland Zanvie and his administrative staff. They were in the administrative offices not many doors away from the negotiating room. The teachers would not let the administrators leave the building.

The lock-in situation created great tension among many people in the community, and the situation was extremely volatile. Especially upset was the high school principal's wife, Mrs. August Fast, an excitable, garrulous woman. She denounced the teachers' tactics and vowed to break the picket line. On the evening of January 12, she drove to the administration building. As she watched the marching teachers on the driveway and the pavement at the administration building — where they were carrying banners and placards and were chanting "Contract, contract, contract," Mrs. Fast was infuriated. Jockeying her car into position, she blew the horn, stuck her head out of the window and shouted, "Get out of the road!" When the picket line didn't move, she drove forward. As the car nosed into the group, several teachers fell to the driveway, and the car actually ran over several teachers.

DISCUSSION QUESTIONS

1. What do you think of the teachers' tactics to resolve the contract dispute?
2. What are the long-range implications of such a breakdown in negotiations?
3. How could the situation have been alleviated?
4. Did the actions of Mrs. Fast improve the climate for negotiations? Explain your response.
5. What legal implications are involved for Mrs. Fast?

Collective Bargaining

Color Me Heavy

Maggie Oates was a ten-year veteran in the Westfield School District. Maggie was considered an adequate teacher by parents in the community, but many were chagrined because each year Maggie grew heavier and heavier. In fact, during her ten years teaching the fourth grade she gained 157 pounds. Currently, Maggie weighed 267!

At the end of the school year, she enrolled in summer school at Eastern University to acquire additional skills and to obtain new ideas. On the campus, Ms. Oates visited the national Bookman's Exhibit. She was excited by the displays and bought books, supplies, and materials she felt she might use in her work in the fall at her grade level. But when she reached her apartment in early August, Ms. Oates read a letter from the personnel office. It advised her of reassignment to a junior high school in a notoriously "tough" neighborhood.

At once, Ms. Oates filed a grievance protesting "unfair labor practices."

DISCUSSION QUESTIONS

1. Does the administration have the prerogative to change an individual's grade level and building?
2. How would you have handled the situation if you were the superintendent of schools? Maggie Oates?
3. What do you feel will be the outcome of the grievance?
4. What should the teacher's contract state regarding the reassignment of teachers?

Heavy Maggie

Collective Bargaining

When You Slip — You Fall

Janet Gretz was the chief negotiator for the Big Mountain School District. She prided herself on being tough and was respected by the administration. During the collective bargaining process, Ms. Gretz negotiated a lucrative financial package for the teachers. The contract also stipulated a reduced class load. She had failed, however, to do anything about teacher attendance on "snow or ice days." Max Jason, the superintendent, had insisted that teachers show up, even if the school buses could not run their routes and students could not attend classes. Although Jason during negotiations had made financial concessions, he refused to yield to the teachers on the "snow days issue." Janet had won a victory in financial matters and agreed grudgingly to the superintendent's stand on inclement weather.

An early ice storm struck in November. Mr. Jason decided that bus operation was unsafe. The local radio station announced school closings and added that teachers were expected to report as usual.

That morning, Janet Gretz got into her Mustang and grumbled to herself every one of the fifteen miles over the ice-covered roads to Foxville Secondary School. The parking lot was a glaze of ice — and not a foot was salted. When she got out of her car, she slipped and fell. She tried to save herself, but her head struck the front bumper of her car. Her glasses shattered. From a seven-inch gash in the back of her head, blood spilled out over her dress.

Upon her recovery, Ms. Gretz filed a grievance. She charged unfair working conditions and sued the board of education for negligence.

DISCUSSION QUESTIONS

1. Do you think the present policy will be changed because of the grievance?
2. Should a teacher who has been injured on school property be allowed to file a grievance?
3. Why do you believe Mr. Jason held out for his position?
4. What would your position have been?

Critical Incidents In School Administration

SELECTED REFERENCES
COLLECTIVE BARGAINING

The American Association of School Administrators. *The School Administrator and Negotiation.*, Washington, D.C., 1968.

Braun, Robert J. *Teachers and Power: The Story of the American Federation of Teachers*, New York, Simon and Schuster, 1972.

Carlton, Patrick W. and Harold Goodwin. *The Collective Dilemma: Negotiations in Education.*, Worthington, Ohio, Charles A. Jones Publishing Co., 1969.

The Department of Elementary School Principals, The National Education Association. *Professional Negotiation and the Principalship*, Washington, D.C., 1969.

Doherty, Robert E. and Walter E. Oberer. *Teachers, School Boards, and Collective Bargaining*, Ithaca, New York State School of Industrial and Labor Relations, 1967.

Gilroy, Thomas P. *Educator's Guide to Collective Negotiations.*, Columbus, Ohio, Charles E. Merrill Publishing Company, 1969.

Koerner, T. F. "What to do When the Bargaining Goes Sour." *American School Board Journal.* 157:21-22, August, 1969.

Lieberman, M. "Advantages and Disadvantages of Joint Bargaining," *School Management,* 15:4-5, July, 1971.

Meyers, Donald A. *Teacher Power, Professionalism and Collective Bargaining*, Lexington, Mass., Lexington Books, 1973.

Michael, Lloyd S. "The Principal and Trends in Professional Negotiations," *National Association of Secondary School Principal's Bulletin.*, 52:105-110, May 1968.

Perry, Charles R. and Wesley A. Wildman. *The Impact of Negotiations in Public Education: The Evidence From the Schools*, Worthington, Ohio, Charles A. Jones Publishing Company, 1970.

Rhodes, Eric F. "The Principals Role in Collective Negotiations," *Educational Service Bureau*, 1967, 1-113.

Shannon, T. A. "Principals' Management Role in Collective Negotiations, Grievances, and Strikes," *Journal of Secondary Education*, 45-51-56, February, 1970.

Shils, Edward B. and Taylor C. Whittier. *Teachers, Administrators and Collective Bargaining*, New York, Thomas Y. Crowell Publishers, 1968.

Stinnett, Timothy M. *Professional Problems of Teachers*, New York, The Mcmillan Company, 1968.

STUDENT REACTION SHEET

INSTRUCTOR _____ STUDENT _____

COURSE _____ DATE _____

CRITICAL INCIDENT _____

REACTION:

REFERENCES CITED

1. _____
2. _____
3. _____
4. _____

Chapter 5

Public Relations

Dealing with people is probably the most important responsibility of any administrator. Research shows that success in most positions is largely due to one's skill in human relations, based upon personality and the ability to lead people. John D. Rockefeller once said, "The ability to deal with people is as purchasable a commodity as sugar or coffee, and I will pay more for that ability than for any other under the sun."

Successful administrators possess, in addition to their knowledge of the profession, the ability to speak effectively, to win people to their way of thinking, and to "sell" themselves and their ideas. Personality and the art of communication are of inestimable value, may be even more important than years of experience and technical knowledge.

Unfortunately, administrators often *fail* because of personal and public relations. Others *fail* because they are unable to interpret their program to their staff and to the community. Still others do not succeed because they are not democratic in decision making. They are unaware that people need to be motivated, and some often do not cultivate and encourage lay participation in the operation of school business. There are cases on record of educators who are paranoiac of people who question the operation of the school.

Public relations affect every person in a community because everyone is a part of the local school district. If one accepts this concept, logic conduces to the idea that a public relations program should strive to reach everyone in the community. "Hit or miss" public relations have no place in the modern school. Hence, an effective public relations system requires careful planning and a thorough knowledge of the community's social structure. No public relations program is established overnight.

Critical Incidents In School Administration

Nor is it a one-man job. Infinite and widespread cooperation is a *sine qua non*.

Positive public relations is one of the keys to a successful school operation, and schoolmen, at all levels, should strive to promote open, positive communication.

Diploma Diplomacy

Cougar was a mountain-top village in eastern Oregon. Cal Rhodes had been the superintendent for seven years; youthful Bill Jacquith, the principal, had held his job for two years. One May day, Cal, breathing a sigh of relief, said:

"Hey, man! Just two more weeks, and we've got it made with another school year behind us."

Bill nodded. "That's true, but we've got three big events ahead of us. There's the honors banquet, baccalaureate, and commencement. Keep your fingers crossed."

Especially as school administrators near the school year's end, hope springs eternal! It had been a good year for the school and both men.

But the morning after the honors banquet, the roof fell in. Bill had thought both the banquet and program had gone off beautifully. As a result, Dorothia Jacks' telephone call really floored him.

"Mr. Jacquith," Mrs. Jacks said with apparent anger, "I was most disappointed at the honors banquet. I've never seen such a high degree of favoritism."

"I'm not sure I know what you mean."

"I mean precisely what I said," she replied — heatedly. "Last year my son George won the most valuable basketball player award, last night he didn't get the award. His father and I felt certain he had a better season this year. He was most certainly the most valuable player on the team!"

"Of course, I'm sorry George did not receive the award," Bill said. "But the players and coaches did the balloting, as you know. The process was the same as last year, and it was completely democratic and fair."

"You'll have to prove that to me, young man. Besides, I've told my son he's done participating in any more school activities. He's only to attend classes, and he will not take part in commencement exercises."

"That's too bad, Mrs. Jacks. I hope you will reconsider, — for your son's sake."

Public Relations

Instantly, Bill reported the details to the superintendent who shrugged. "They're a strange family."

Until three days before commencement, no more was heard from the Jacks family. Then, young George visited the principal's office. "I have a job lined up over in Tiverton, and I can start today. School's out and I need the job. The foreman over there said that I'm the best qualified of all the applicants, but he needs verification that I have graduated. He promised, if I'd bring my diploma to work in the morning, he'd give me the job. Otherwise, it goes to someone else."

"I'm sorry, George," said Mr. Jacquith, "our policy is to present the diplomas at commencement exercises. Come to commencement Sunday afternoon and receive yours like all the rest."

"You know I can't do that," said George. He stalked out of the principal's office.

Within ten minutes, George's mother stormed into the office demanding a copy of her son's diploma.

Mr. Rhodes, the superintendent, enforced the school's policy and Bill's decision. That same evening board president Hank Werstler telephoned. He said the administration's intransigence was causing all kinds of bad vibrations in the community.

"All over town, this thing is being blown out of proportion," Mr. Werstler said. "We've got to put the lid on. Let's have a meeting and discuss the situation."

DISCUSSION QUESTIONS

1. What alternatives are left for the board of education and administrators of Cougar?
2. Should Mrs. Jacks be forced to allow George to attend commencement exercises with all the other graduates?
3. Is the present policy of the board and administration fair?
4. What public relations problems does a policy like this cause within a community?

The Not So Vanishing Vandal

Enroute to his office early one morning, Superintendent Bill Rapp looked at the new high school next to the administration building. Bill was proud of the five million dollar edifice. He felt pretty good that, as a second-year administrator, he had supervised the passage of a bond issue. Several times before Bill's arrival, three bond issues had been turned down. Each time he looked at the high school, he knew that the community of Monkton had an outstanding facility. It was a functional and educationally sound structure, and it was open until 10:00 p.m., Monday through Friday, and all day Saturday.

But that morning something was different about the building. He couldn't put his finger on it, however, and forgot it.

At 7:45 a.m., as he was dictating letters, the telephone rang. "Good morning, Bill. This is Tom Phillips. I hate to tell you this, but we've got a real problem at the high school. All the first floor windows are busted. All the hallway walls are covered with paint. It's a mess. You better come over right away."

Tom Phillips was the dependable, well-liked principal of Monkton High, and his phone call initiated the most traumatic day in Superintendent Rapp's life.

As he hurried towards the high school, he wondered why, earlier, he had not noticed that every window pane was gone!

At the main entrance to the high school, Tom Phillips met him. "Bill, this is awful. It's the worst case of vandalism I've ever seen or even heard about. Damage will run into thousands of dollars."

"Well, let's go have a look, Tom. I might as well face the music now as later. We better call the board president. You have any idea who did it?"

Tom shook his head.

Bill made a quick tour of the building and tried to estimate the damage. Then he headed back to his office. He must contact Warren Figg, board president, at once.

Mr. Figg was the most influential and wealthy man in the county. A descendant of early settlers, he owned vast tracts of real estate which had been in the family for generations. Mr. Figg, by subdividing some acreage, had increased the family wealth.

A public spirited citizen, he had spent much money and used his influence in building the new high school. His only child was in tenth grade, and Mr. Figg wanted the lad to have the best possible education.

Just as he was about to call Mr. Figg, the phone rang. He had visions of newspaper reporters writing up the story. Reluctantly, he picked up the instrument and said: "Bill Rapp speaking." In the long silence, Bill was nonplused. Then, he said again, "This is Bill Rapp speaking." As if from some distance a voice said, "You want to know who wrecked the school? Just ask Curtis Figg." The line clicked dead.

Bill said to himself, "What the devil?" Then, he began to ponder: Did the caller mean that Curtis Figg knew who did it? Did it mean that Curtis was the ring leader of a gang who did do the vandalism? Or was the inference that Curtis did it by himself? Or was some jealous person envious of the Figg's position in the community falsely blaming Curtis Figg?

What hopes Curt's dad had for the boy! What dreams! Well, the situation would have to be handled with infinite tact. Certainly, Figg, Sr., could not believe his son could do anything wrong, let alone maliciously damage the school. Good heavens, what a tangled mess. Bill Rapp reached for the phone. He hated to think of talking to Warren Figg, the board president.

DISCUSSION QUESTIONS
1. What procedure would you follow to ascertain those to blame?
2. How would you approach Curtis? His father?
3. Should the police be contacted before anything else was done?
4. As president of the board of education, Mr. Figg should be called immediately; should the superintendent mention anything about the anonymous telephone call to him?

The Last Tatto

Millstream, a community of 7,000 inhabitants lies a few miles from the Skyline Drive in North Carolina. Throughout its history, the community had sent many of its young men to wars. Beginning with the Civil War and through the Vietnam conflict, Millstream's youth had served their country. In the city park, near the center of town, statues and tablets depicting regional and local feats reminded passersby of the town's glory.

Felix Mander, sixty year old commander of the local militia, was a proud veteran of World War II. He had seen action in various European campaigns. He wore on his military uniform several decorations gained through meritorious action in battle. Felix also supported community causes and had served for years as a member of the Millstream Board of Education.

Critical Incidents In School Administration

The month of May was near, and to Felix that month invariably was busy. The annual Memorial Day Celebration was one of Millstream's — and the county's — major events.

One evening in April, Felix was listing the events for the Memorial Day Program. Certainly, he thought, the Millstream Marching Band would lead the parade, and Joe Constable, the first chair trumpet player, would sound taps at the cemetery.

But the old warrior had miscalculated. Mr. Cecil Rice, the youthful, first-year band director, had his own ideas. His band had been successful under his baton. It had placed first in the district, regional, and state contests in various solo and ensemble competitions; band members had done very well. Unfortunately, the state finals for school musicians were scheduled on the day following Millstream's Memorial Day tribute! Young Mr. Rice knew that twenty of the seventy members of the band were to participate in the contests. It would be difficult for them to take part also in the local festivities. They would be tired, and he doubted that they could perform capably at the Music Festival in Durham.

Both Mr. Mander and Mr. Rice were on a collision course. Unfortunately, Mr. Mander was shocked when he called Mr. Rice to confirm the long-standing community tradition.

Mr. Rice explained his position, and Mr. Mander explained his thoughts. In the discussion, Mr. Mander told Mr. Rice the band would perform at the Memorial Day Ceremony no matter what. He also advised the music director that Mr. Jameson, the superintendent, would hear about the problem.

DISCUSSION QUESTIONS

1. Should Mr. Mander, as a board member, be supported by the superintendent?
2. Should the excellent young band director, Mr. Rice, be supported by the superintendent?
3. How could a compromise settlement be developed between Mr. Rice and Mr. Mander?
4. Should Mr. Rice have been made aware of the community's tradition before the April confrontation?
5. What should the school policy be regarding the participation of school students in community events?

Public Relations

A Trip Gone to Pot

Each June, the St. Mary's High School graduating class enjoyed a senior trip to the nation's capitol. John Henry — the happy-go-lucky shop teacher and perennial senior adviser — and his wife always had accompanied the thirty members of the small senior class. It was a week-long tour and the graduating class looked forward to it. Funds for the trip were raised by candy sales, car washes, and locally gathered maple syrup sales. The itinerary called for a visit with the district congressman and sightseeing at the White House, the Washington Monument, the Jefferson and Lincoln memorials, Ford Theatre, the FBI building, and other points of attraction. The group traveled by bus and stayed at the Lincoln Travel Inn, in nearby Alexandria.

The senior classes of the past had been generally well-behaved, and serious problems were almost non-existent. But this year's expedition caused Mr. and Mrs. Henry some apprehension. In the past two months, two underclassmen had been caught smoking pot in the restroom, and a third student was sufficiently "spaced out" to require hospital attention.

Prior to departure, Mr. Henry and the high school principal, Sam Jones, met with the group and reiterated the rules and regulations. They stressed the fact that the students themselves were responsible for their behavior and that the outcome of this trip would affect future senior trips. Among the various good conduct regulations were the following:

1. No drugs.
2. No alcohol.
3. Good bus behavior.
4. Curfew at 11:00 p.m.
5. No member of the opposite sex in hotel rooms after 9:30 p.m.
6. Good restaurant behavior.

During the planning stages, all went well. Schedules were developed, money was raised, and the bus trip to Washington was pleasant.

By the third day in the city, Mr. and Mrs. Henry breathed a sigh of relief. Everything was perfect. Thursday morning at 2:15, however, Mr. and Mrs. Henry were awakened from a sound sleep by loud knocking on their motel bedroom door. At the door stood two Alexandria policemen.

"Are you Mr. and Mrs. Henry, the St. Mary's chaperones for seniors?" The larger of the two policemen snarled out the question.

"Yes, sir. Anything wrong?"

"You bet you," said the other officer. "A boy named John Jacobson says he's one of your students. He was arrested in a crosstown bar for trying to sell marijuana to a plainclothes detective. We've got him at the station house now. He says he's innocent, but we got the goods. He was caught red-handed."

"Give me a minute to get dressed."

As Mr. Henry closed the door, he shook his head sorrowfully and said to his wife, "Mary, how will we ever explain this to the superintendent, to John's parents, and to the community?"

DISCUSSION QUESTIONS

1. Of what value are senior trips?
2. As an administrator, how would you handle this problem within the community?
3. Should one student's actions jeopardize future senior trips?
4. Could Mr. and Mrs. Henry have done anything to prevent this incident from happening?
5. Is the district liable for the actions of students on senior trips?

Thirty Pieces of Silver

The Mohawk County football team had just completed the last game of the season. Played on the Justin High School field, the game was closely contested, with Mohawk County making its first loss to undefeated Justin High by a score of 13-7. A halfback reverse in the third quarter proved Mohawk's undoing as the Justin High runner had raced 68 yards for a touchdown. When the team poured out of the locker room and into the yellow Mohawk County bus, the coach slapped each player on the back in an expression of condolence. With the weary, crestfallen players in the bus, Mr. James, the head football coach, made a quiet speech.

"Let me tell you, fellows. You played your hearts out tonight. Except for one lapse in our secondary, we'd have won. You know Mr. Samuel Brooks back home said, if you won, he'd finance a victory celebration at Sampson's, that snazzy restaurant here in Justin. I know you don't feel like a big celebration, but both Mr. Brooks and I agree that you deserve a feast anyhow. We're going to stop at Sampson's anyway before we go home. Mr. Brooks told me that you can order from the menu. Anything you want. Let's forget the game and let's eat!"

Public Relations

The squad whistled and clapped their approval. In a few minutes, the bus was filled with conversation and good-natured banter.

Dinner over, the team again boarded the bus for the seventy mile trip home. Ten miles from Justin, Coach James noted that the bus was slowing down. "Something wrong with the bus?" The driver answered at once. "We've got two police cars coming up behind us lickety-split. They got their flashers a-turning. They're in a big hurry. I thought I'd pull over and let them pass."

Coach James settled back in his seat. But he heard the bus driver gasp, "Holy gee! They're after us. I wasn't speeding. What's going on?"

A Justin policeman clambered abroad the school bus.

"Sorry to stop you," he said. "But the owner of Sampson's restaurant is missing some silverware. He has an idea some of your boys swiped it. I'm afraid if it isn't handed over, I'll have to search the bus."

When Coach James arose to speak to the team, he saw the reporter from the *Daily Times* taking notes. There would be bad publicity for the team and school. It was exactly ten years before that the football team got in hot water for drinking alcoholic beverages on the bus after a game. "Well, here we go again," Mr. James muttered.

DISCUSSION QUESTIONS

1. If the accusation were true, how would you as a coach handle the situation?
2. If the accusation were false, how would you as a coach handle it?
3. If the accusation were true, as an administrator, how would you handle this situation within the community?
4. How would you discipline those responsible?

The Zebra Complex

Morton was an all-white rural community located 60 miles from the nearest metropolitan area. The high school was a member of the tri-county B League which included other rural communities and one urban high school. Morton's all-white citizenry had had only one association with blacks. That came in its activity participation with Ridge High, predominantly black.

Critical Incidents In School Administration

Although the two schools had competed for five years in various ways with few misunderstandings or incidents, the basketball games were developing tension. Last year the teams played three times: twice in the regular season and once at the regional finals in Lancaster of which Ridge was a suburb. The teams divided in the regular season. In the regional, Ridge defeated Morton by one point and won the crown. At each game, isolated incidents occurred. Once a crisis almost developed when Morton fans left the regional finals. There were jeers and jostling on both sides. Small group fights flared, but the riot-tested Lancaster police maintained order.

Before the first game of the current season, several letters to the editor in Morton argued that Morton fans and players should not have to put up with the blacks from Ridge. Several correspondents hinted that athletic contests and relationships should be terminated. Morton's Superintendent Carlson defended the contests and association as good learning situations for the middle-class white students of the local school. He wrote his opinions in a letter to the newspaper and cited the need for the two schools to share cultural activities. The Morton School Board defended the superintendent's recommendation that athletic events and other high school activities be continued.

That year, both high schools had fine basketball seasons, and during regular season's play no serious incidents developed. Once more, though, another regional showdown was in the making. The difference, this year, however, was that the game was scheduled at the spacious fieldhouse of the regional university located between Morton and Ridge.

The battle was nip and tuck almost to the final whistle. During the game, jeers and catcalls from both sides of the fieldhouse punctuated the excitement. In the last second, Morton won by a single point. Some Ridge fans, upset and emotional, ran across the court to the Morton bleachers. Here and there, fights broke out. Many Morton students, trying to avoid the fisticuffs, jumped off the bleachers and sprained ankles and wrists.

Police and calmer citizens quelled the riot in 15 minutes. Scores of fans and policemen were injured. The next evening in both communities newspapers blamed each other. Morton's citizens were outraged at the violence. Ridge's citizens were angered by what they considered unfair refereeing and racial taunts. Almost endless letters reached the editors in both communities; board members met and scolded the other community!

Public Relations

DISCUSSION QUESTIONS

1. Should relations between the two schools be discontinued? Why?
2. Should they be continued? Why?
3. What type of positive public relations programs could be utilized?
4. What can be done to alleviate the problem between the two schools? The two communities?
5. What procedures might have been utilized to prevent this occurrence from happening after the game?

Too Close for Comfort

Baggitt High School was located one block from the downtown area. A small community with many retirees, the town was growing slowly. Conservative by nature, community leaders fought the invasion of heavy industry. They wanted to preserve the tranquility of historically preserved Baggitt, the population of which had increased only by 2,000 since 1900.

The high school was considered excellent and was a source of great community pride. The school was surrounded by a lower middle class neighborhood, with some small business and professional offices. With the exception of the main street, located a block north, the school was in a residential area. But the location caused a problem.

The high school's hot lunch program was designed to serve the growing number of youngsters bussed in from rural areas. However, many students enjoyed eating at two accessible short-order grills. "George's," a typical greasy spoon, was opposite the school's main entrance, and the "Dug Out," another favorite, was located a block away. When the third hour or lunch-break bell sounded, students hustled to the "four winds." Some sped to the cafeteria to be first in line. Others raced to "George's" or the "Dug Out." Others dashed home for lunch.

Both George and the owner of the "Dug Out," Red Blaine, welcomed the high school trade. They specialized in short orders, and most students ordered the traditional hamburger, fries and a malt.

Unfortunately, old Mrs. Dubbins and her next door neighbor, a Mr. Tucker, paid a high price as the students dashed to the grills. The flow of

George's Hot Lunch Special

Public Relations

traffic literally crossed the citizens' properties. Students made paths in the grass, stoved in picket fences, and threw napkins, french fry dishes, and milk shake containers all over the lawns. The private property was a constant mess.

In despair, Mr. Tucker and Mrs. Dubbins circulated a petition among their neighbors. It asked school officials to make "George's" and the "Dug Out" off limits to students during the noon hour.

When the owners got wind of the petition, they attended the school board meeting to protest. Both they and other downtown merchants claimed the petition challenged private enterprise.

The administration and Baggitt Board of Education faced a dilemma. How should the issue be resolved?

DISCUSSION QUESTIONS

1. Should students be prohibited from frequenting the two short-order restaurants?
2. Should a school official monitor the environment during the noon hour?
3. Should George and Red Blaine hire individuals to clean up and repair any damage to the Dubbins and Tucker properties?
4. What is your position on an open campus?

Too Much Too Early

Midwestern University placed senior teacher-trainees in student teaching positions in Else, a community 30 miles away. Believing that it was wise to cluster a number of student teachers within one building in a particular semester, the university administrators assigned between 10-14 student teachers at the high school of 2,000 students. The university leaders sold the Else Board of Education, the administration and the teacher's organization the belief that student teachers could be highly beneficial to classroom teachers. The neophytes would provide regular teachers with released time to visit other schools to see innovative and interesting programs and to do curriculum and other preparatory work for their classrooms. It was also suggested that under proper conditions the student teachers might substitute for their classroom supervising teachers.

Critical Incidents In School Administration

The University provided a full-time university supervisor to monitor and aid the classroom teachers and building administrators by being in the building two days per week and on call throughout the semester. Both institutions liked the arrangement. Student teachers actually provided extra help to the regular teachers and enabled considerably more time to individual attention for students.

In the second year of the arrangement, Superintendent William Hawkes began receiving telephone calls from concerned parents. They were concerned that the students were not having enough access to the regularly certified teachers. Classes too frequently were being "turned over" to "practice teachers" while the regular teachers shirked their teaching responsibilities and were "never available." One parent charged that her son in six periods had five student teachers.

Initially, the superintendent minimized the complaints, but at the December board of education meeting, a petition signed by 80 concerned parents was presented to him. It requested that student teachers not be assigned to Else High School.

DISCUSSION QUESTIONS

1. What should the board of education do to correct the situation?
2. How should the superintendent react to the parents?
3. What is the role of the building principal?
4. What should be the role of the university supervisor?
5. What should be the role of the classroom teacher, the student teacher?
6. Is there any value in having a cooperative student teaching program between a teacher education institution and a public or parochial school system?

SELECTED REFERENCES
PUBLIC RELATIONS

Campbell, C. C. "P. R. For Public Schools," *School and Community,* 60:17 October, 1973.

Dapper, Gloria. *Public Relations For Educators,* New York, The Macmillan Co., 1968.

Filbin, R. "Do Superintendents Spend Enough Time on Public Relations?" *Phi Delta Kappan,* 53:193, November, 1971.

Henderson, George. *Human Relations: From Theory to Practice,* Tulsa, Oklahoma, The University of Oklahoma Press, 1974.

Hilton, E. "A Little Image Polishing Might Help," *Instructor,* 83:12, October, 1973.

Stanford, Gene and Albert E. Roark. *Human Interaction in Education,* Rockleigh, New Jersey: Longwood Division, Allyn and Bacon, Inc., 1971.

STUDENT REACTION SHEET

INSTRUCTOR _____ STUDENT _____

COURSE _____ DATE _____

CRITICAL INCIDENT _____

REACTION:

_____

_____

_____

_____

_____

_____

_____

_____

_____

_____

_____

_____

_____

_____

_____

_____

_____

_____

REFERENCES CITED

1. _____
2. _____
3. _____
4. _____

Chapter 6

Extra Curricular Activities

The value of most extra curricular activities in a school cannot be disputed. Athletics, special interest clubs, class organizations, homerooms, student publications, student councils, and social affairs tend to supplement the academic program at all levels.

In the elementary grades, after-school recreation programs offer instruction in various sports and musical skills. School bands and orchestras and art training may begin after school. If over a period of time continued interest develops, these activities may become part of the regular school curriculum.

In the middle school and high school, extra curricular activities are generally more organized and varied. Groups are formed in areas ranging from agriculture to zoology. Programs such as competitive athletics are not only much more widespread but also better organized and funded than the elementary school activities. Great variety is found within a school and also between schools.

One school's activities may consist of class organizations and a football team; another may consist of thirty or forty separate student organizations.

Most students benefit from extra curricular activities by developing knowledge, skills, and attitudes relevant to them then and later in life. Other students may find an extra curricular area unavailable to them in the regular offerings. They may "do very poorly in school" yet excel in and learn much from extra curricular pursuits. Considerable numbers have even found involvement in extra curricular activities a primary factor in the decision to remain in school.

Extra curricular activities have been prized from the times of the ancient Greeks who included running and exercising as an integral part of their education. Thus, the modern administrator should attempt to generate and maintain activities which fill the needs of the student, the community, and society in general. Such programs foster administrative problems that may be vexing. Some of the questions school administrators must seek to answer are the following:

Who should set policies regarding the extra curricular activities?

Should all activities occur during the school day?

How much should sponsors be paid?

How often should extra curricular activities be offered?

How is an extra curricular program financed?

Should every teacher be included in the extra curricular program?

Who assigns sponsors to extra curricular activities?

Is tenure a factor in sponsoring an extra curricular activity?

Should an accountability factor be employed in evaluating an extra curricular activity?

Who is responsible for the success or failure of an extra curricular program?

These and many other questions are relevant to the schoolman who seeks to offer a well-balanced and meaningful program.

The Ghost Writer

The White Clarion, White Bluffs High School newspaper, had just published its last issue of the year. Mrs. Franks, the faculty sponsor, had approved the articles one week earlier, and the student editor had delivered the proofs to the printer. When the newspaper appeared, several "substituted" articles were derogatory to administrators, teachers, and students alike. One essay equated Mr. Wise, the assistant principal, with Hitler. The math teacher, Miss Wysong, was pictured as a snow flake. Several popular athletes were described as muscular morons who received special favors.

Mr. Wise summoned Mrs. Franks to his office at once. "Mrs. Franks," he said, "it appears that we have a problem. Parents and board members are angry. Several faculty members are displeased with the newspaper, and a good many students are upset. This issue isn't consistent with your past standards."

Extra Curricular Activities

"I'm flabbergasted, Mr. Wise!" exclaimed Mrs. Franks. "We followed the regular publication procedure. Articles were approved last week, and the student editor took the copy to the printer. I had no idea that new articles were substituted for approved ones. Some students must have done this."

"It's too late now to do anything about today's paper, but we can tighten up our supervision so that this situation never occurs again. What can we do to be sure about it?"

DISCUSSION QUESTIONS

1. Who is ultimately responsible for articles published in school newspapers?
2. What steps might be taken to rectify the current situation?
3. What should the assistant principal and the faculty sponsor do to reprimand the guilty students?
4. What controls should the school district place on student publications?

Soft Revolution

The student council at Redeemer High School had always been an integral part of school life. Its membership was composed of representatives from each of the certain school clubs and organizations. Interest ran high in student government this year. During the campaigns for student council offices, the officers had attended a state training session for student council representatives, and the young people returned with some new ideas and policies.

Billy Wagner, student council president, made the following speech to the council: "Friends, I've been attending the State Student Government Conference, and I've got some recommendations I'd like you to consider:

1. The faculty sponsor must be elected by the student council and be approved by the principal.
2. The student council will negotiate a budget with the board of education.
3. The student council will have one day during the year to offer a workshop for students.

4. The principal may not issue a new policy regarding student behavior or control without approval from the student council."

"I believe it's time we student representatives make some demands. This is our school, and our parents' money pays for our education."

The students were extremely excited. "Wow, Billy's right on," said Amy. "It's about time we *really do* something around here."

"Hey, man," said Frankie, "I really dig it. Let's get behind our man. We'll make a lot of difference around here."

Later that afternoon Father Keane called Billy into his office. "Billy, my boy, you're a fine lad," he said. "Why, I've known you from boyhood, and your father and mother were my first students. I want to ask you a question, son. Why stir up all this trouble?"

"Well, sir, I don't mean to be disrespectful, but we think it's time the student council really does something positive for the school. We make a big thing of the election process. Then what? Not much, sir. We have a lot of meetings, run a big cleanup campus campaign, and throw a few dances. Excuse me, but aren't schools for kids? Where would the teachers be without us? So, I don't see why the governing body of the students can't have something to say about what really happens to us."

DISCUSSION QUESTIONS

1. As the principal, how would you reply to Billy?
2. What would you do to help Billy redefine the student council role?
3. How important is a student council to a school?
4. What is the role of a student council in setting, implementing, and evaluating school policy?
5. What areas of policy should be under student council jurisdiction? Explain your response.

All in the Family

Jim Barber, a junior in high school, was very active in extra curricular activities. He was a member of the student council, hall monitor, soloist in the choir, a three-sport participant, and a member of the principal's advisory council. He had found success in these activities which satisfied

Extra Curricular Activities

many of his high school needs. However, Jim began neglecting his regular subjects. He was failing one course and barely passing the others.

Since the school policy about athletic eligibility stated eligibility loss to a student failing more than one subject, Jim was upset.

Several teachers and the counselor discussed the problem with him. Mr. Martin, the biology teacher, said, "Jim, you've got to buckle down. You are barely passing. If you fail the lab practical, you'll fail the class. What's the problem?"

"I'm just not getting the material, Mr. Martin. I have so many things happening now that I can't concentrate on anything. I'll try harder."

Mrs. Snow, the counselor told Jim the following: "I know you really enjoy your outside activities, but you're carrying more than you can handle right now. What are we to do about it? Perhaps it would be best if you dropped at *least* one activity."

"You're right, Mrs. Snow. I am having trouble in biology . . ."

"Now, Jim, you know it's more than biology," Mrs. Snow replied.

"You're right, Mrs. Snow," said Jim. "I guess I am in a little deep right now. But I don't know what to do. All the kids look up to me. And when I mention quitting they really get up tight. I sure hate to get the kids mad at me, you know? Well, I gotta go now. I have a meeting. Bye, Mrs. Snow."

A week after the meeting, Mrs. Snow noted that Jim was following all his usual pursuits. When she called his parents, they said their son had the right to make up his own mind. They were proud of Jim's extra curricular achievements and dismissed his academic problems with, "Oh, well, neither his father nor I were much for studies ourselves."

DISCUSSION QUESTIONS

1. Should schools limit the number of extra curricular activities a student may participate in?
2. If a student is not performing well in the classroom, does the school have the legal right and/or moral responsibility to remove a student from extra curricular activities?
3. Are the purposes of extra curricular activities being served correctly in the Jim Barber case?
4. What responsibility does the principal have in setting extra curricular activity policy?

Critical Incidents In School Administration

The Old Sports Super Boosters

The North Beach Public School District had a history of defeated millage elections. Each year the board contemplated which economies should come next: teachers or programs. In the current year, meetings were controversial and heated. At its last meeting the board members voted 5 to 4 to drop all extra curricular activities including interscholastic athletics. Until another millage election was voted on successfully, that situation would continue.

The public reaction was prompt and predictable. Citizens were outraged! A recall petition was discussed, and a student walk-out was feared. However, the board stood by its unpopular decision. "For years," the board president stated, "we have cut and pared our educational program. We have no other alternatives now. It's no more frills. So it's up to you, the citizens."

The athletic booster club called a special meeting to try to solve the problem. Charles Vincent, a local businessman, made a key speech.

"Friends, the athletic program has always been strong, and we've had our share of winning and even championship teams. I can't imagine all the negative effects if we don't have athletic teams next year. I sure know some of them. North Beach will lose its place in the athletic conference. Our children won't be eligible for scholarships, and a lot of kids won't know what to do with themselves after school. And there's the loss of community pride. Damn it, we've got to convince the board to find other alternatives to solve this money problem."

Jerry Muny, the local doctor, said, "Our kids need athletics. It's possible we could even be state champs next year in football. I have an idea. Let's start a North Beach Sports Fund. We'll go after private donations to finance the athletic program. I'll donate the first $500 to kick off the campaign."

In a month's time, $30,000 was raised, and Mr. Vincent attended a board meeting to present the check in support of the athletic program.

Extra Curricular Activities

> **DISCUSSION QUESTIONS**
> 1. What kind of a precedent is set if the board accepts the funds from the athletic booster club?
> 2. What other options did the board have instead of cutting the extra curricular program?
> 3. If the board accepts the locally solicited funds, should it be used to finance only the athletic program or all extra curricular programs?
> 4. Should a committee be formed to resolve the problem of community relations?

Good Intentions — Tough Sentence

Kendall High's senior class had been working for four years raising money for a class trip to Washington. They sold coat hangers, baked goods, school pride buttons, and candy, and had sponsored film series and collected tickets at school dances and ball games.

The class president, Gary Jones, and vice-president, Bill Williams, hoped to earn some extra money for the class by charging visiting students admission to junior high school basketball games. The junior high policy, however, was to grant free admission to all students.

When Mr. Mills, the high school principal, learned of the plans, he summoned the boys to his office. "Hi, fellows. I heard a rumor you charged a twenty-five cent admission price to visiting students at last week's junior high game."

"Gee, Mr. Mills, I don't remember anything like that," Gary Jones replied.

"Well, several Cope Junior High students said that you charged admission and put the money in the senior class fund. I want to know the truth. If you didn't, I'll have to find out what the students meant."

"Okay, okay, Mr. Mills. We didn't think it would harm anyone. Besides our school is the only one that doesn't charge admission to the junior high school games. Well, we charged twenty-five cents, sure enough, for the class. We only made $2.50, and we'll be glad to pay it back," Gary said. Both boys were embarrassed.

Critical Incidents In School Administration

"I'm glad you told the truth. I'm not sure what happens next. Just sit tight until I talk with the superintendent about the matter," Mr. Mills said.

Later Mr. Mills told the boys that he and the superintendent agreed that the boys might not participate in any extra curricular activity for one week. In addition, they had to resign their leadership positions in the senior class and send $2.50 and a letter of apology to the Cope Junior High School principal. Finally the boys were to remain in the after-school study hall for one week.

DISCUSSION QUESTIONS

1. Did the punishment fit the crime in this case study?
2. Should an infraction of the rules in an extra curricular activity affect academic work and vice versa?
3. Can you suggest a different procedure for solving this problem?
4. Do schools place too much emphasis on extra curricular activities?
5. What happens to an administrator's credibility when he overreacts in an atmosphere of confidence?

March Madness

March Madness is tournament time in basketball, and it brings a range of emotions. Joy, sorrow, fear, and anxiety run rampant in the school halls, and this year that was the state of affairs at Muladore High School. The boys' basketball team was in the regional finals against crosstown rival St. Mary's. The town was as taut as the student bodies.

Two nights before the finals, St. Mary's was vandalized. Someone painted a skull and crossbones on the front door. The next night Muladore High's emblem — a bull — disappeared. A scrawny-looking chicken replaced the totem. The day of the game sporadic street fights broke out. Rumors were rampant about more to come. The situation was extremely serious. The result: a hastily called meeting of both school boards. The board members drew up a statement. It was read to students and released to the news media:

> "We, the governing boards of Muladore and St. Mary's high schools, have decided to close tonight's game to all spectators.

Extra Curricular Activities

Fearing for the players' and spectators' safety, we regret that this decision has to be made. The game will be taped and shown at a delayed broadcast."

Both students and citizens were irate. Around town the comments were numerous and varied: "My son is playing tonight. I should be allowed to go." "The pep band has worked up some special numbers. It's not fair to ban us." "I've bought tickets. They'll probably keep my money too." "The troublemakers ruin it for the rest of us." "There will be lots more trouble now." "The kids at St. Mary's are always making trouble for us." "The kids at Muladore blame us for everything."

DISCUSSION QUESTIONS

1. What factors do you think the boards discussed before deciding on closing the game to spectators?
2. What's the rationale for competition in extra curricular activities?
3. What other options did the school district have instead of closing the game to spectators?
4. What steps might have been taken prior to the game to solve the violence problem?

Blowing Your Own Horn

Mark Edwards, the band director, stimulated so much enthusiasm in his fine musical program that the band had doubled in size over the past two years. A key to his success was his devotion to his students. Practice sessions were held before and after school, and he gave private lessons on weekends and holidays. Mark also was initiating a new drum and bugle corps. Naturally many of his students were in his organizations.

All was not sweetness and light, however. At a board of education meeting, some parents presented a list of "concerns" regarding Mr. Mark Edwards.

To the principal, Dan Doan, fell the responsibility for an explanation to the hapless musician. "Mark, several parents complained at the board meeting Monday about your small group and private lesson procedures. They think they should not have to pay for lessons, particularly if the practice sessions are in preparation for a school function. They also objected to your private tutoring sessions being held on school property and using school equipment."

"Gee, Mr. Doan," Mark retorted, "I've never held a private lesson during school hours. My private lessons are to improve the skills of individual students. I use the school facilities because they're quiet. Besides, sometimes we need to use special equipment in the band room. When I'm asked to give up my free time, I feel I should be paid for it."

"Are you using the school's equipment and music for your drum and bugle corps? The parents said you were."

"Yes, but I didn't think it would make any difference. I used a little equipment on weekends or after school. The students aren't using it then."

"It looks like we've got a problem, Mark. I think the board will establish a policy in the matter that will solve the problem."

DISCUSSION QUESTIONS

1. What should the school district's policy be concerning use of school facilities and equipment for private purposes?
2. Should faculty be allowed to offer private tutoring for pay? If so, what should be the policy regarding this activity?
3. What role should the principal play regarding parent allegations against a faculty member?
4. Should the industrial arts teacher be allowed to use the school equipment on his own time?

A Railroad Job

Principal Betty Sumac of Deerfield Elementary School was vitally interested in meeting the needs of the students and the community. In view of that, she arranged for a variety of before-and-after-school classes in weaving, drama, ballet, and baton-twirling. After these classes ran for a few months, they were disbanded. One day Miss Sumac had a discussion with Miss Perkins, a first-year teacher.

"How are you enjoying your work?" the principal asked. "I discovered one thing during my first few years. It was that I needed some relaxing outlet. What are your hobbies?"

Extra Curricular Activities

"I was a gymnast in college. I've been working out a few nights a week at the YWCA," the teacher replied.

"That's great! It must be a relaxing way to spend your time. You know that reminds me. Several parents expressed an interest in a tumbling program. You're just the person at the school to sponsor such an activity. With your background and interest you'd get a lot of students. Why don't I put up a sign-up sheet? I'll schedule the first class for one week from today, say at 3:00 in the gym. Isn't it exciting?" Miss Sumac smiled broadly.

"I'm really sorry, Miss Sumac. Two days a week after school I'm pretty well committed. But . . . ."

"Oh, no problem. We'll get it rolling. Of course, we can't pay you for your time. But when you see the girls perform at the Spring Conclave for Parents, it'll be worth every minute of your time. Good luck, Miss Perkins; keep me informed about your progress." Miss Sumac disappeared into her office.

DISCUSSION QUESTIONS

1. Do you agree with the principal's approach in soliciting an activity sponsor or do you think the principal could have used a different method?
2. Is it fair for a teacher to work in an activity and receive no compensation?
3. What is the role of extra curricular activities in an elementary school?
4. What are the personal and educational benefits of a public exhibition of skills?

Add Out?

Mr. Tretorn's tennis team was closing out a winning season. Both his number one singles player, Tommy Love, and the doubles team had qualified for the state tournament. The high school had, almost, in its grasp its first state champions. Mr. Tretorn was excited at the prospect.

The principal complimented Mr. Tretorn on his success and suggested that the team was responsible for the student body's renewed school spirit and pride that spring.

Critical Incidents In School Administration

But two days before the state tournament, Mr. Schultz, president of the school board, stopped to see Mr. Tretorn.

"I'm sorry," Mr. Schultz began. "I've got bad news. Last night at a downtown restaurant, I saw your Tommy Love having a drink."

Although the news knocked the coach for a loop, he said he appreciated the information and would talk to Tom.

"But your training rules state that drinking is grounds for automatic dismissal from the team. Isn't that so?"

"Yes, sir, Mr. Schultz. I promise I'll take care of this situation."

That afternoon the coach talked with Tommy Love. "Were you drinking last night?"

"Yes, coach," Tom answered. "It was Mother's birthday. We had a family celebration at The Inn. You know I'm almost 18, so Dad bought me a drink. Anyway, the drink helped me to relax."

"Suppose, Tom, that you were the coach and your star player broke a training rule. What would you do?"

Tom looked at the coach as if he did not know what to say.

DISCUSSION QUESTIONS

1. What action should the coach, Mr. Tretorn, take regarding his star tennis player?
2. What effect would Tommy Love's dismissal have on the student body and the community?
3. What part should the principal play in matters such as this?
4. Why establish rules and regulations for extra curricular activities?
5. Can school districts establish rules for extra curricular activities that apply to students during the summer months and during vacation periods?

Too Many Irons . . .

At Tuscola High, 250 students were enrolled in grades 9-12. Because the school was small, students could participate in several extra curricular activities. The leaders in one activity frequently were the leaders in several others. Pam Richards was a good example. Head cheerleader, first

How can I play, jump and shoot all at the same time?

chair trumpet section of the band, secretary of the student council, and top scorer on the girls' basketball team, she was also an all-A student.

But her multiple pursuits led to serious conflicts. The next weekend promised endless confusion. She was to play in the regional band contest and the district basketball final. She was to lead cheers at the varsity basketball game. Every activity was scheduled for Saturday!

Jacob Martin, the band director, reminded her that the band really needed her. He added, "Don't forget to practice your solo. We're counting on you."

The girls' basketball coach called Pam out of class and said, "I understand that there's a band contest Saturday. I feel bad for Mr. Martin. You know the district tournament begins Saturday, and you're our best player. With you on the team, we're in the state tournament for the first time. We've got a real opportunity to get to the finals. Be ready, Pam."

Jill St. James, another cheerleader, confided in Pam. "You know I'm not going to the band festival Saturday. The boys need our cheerleading at their game. By the way, what are you going to do?"

Pam was bewildered. There were too many options — really too many genuine obligations.

What should she do?

DISCUSSION QUESTIONS

1. Can you suggest a solution for Pam in the above case study?
2. Should the principal play a role in situations like Pam's?
3. Is it possible for a student to participate successfully in more than one extra curricular activity at a time?
4. What could have been done earlier to avoid such a conflict for Pam Richards?

STUDENT REACTION SHEET

INSTRUCTOR _____ STUDENT _____

COURSE _____ DATE _____

CRITICAL INCIDENT _____

REACTION:

REFERENCES CITED

1.
2.
3.
4.

SELECTED REFERENCES
EXTRA CURRICULAR ACTIVITIES

"Are Activities Programs Really Activities Programs?," *School Activities,* Number 39, September 1967.

Armstrong, R. L. "Student Council: Whither Goest Thou?," *Clearing House,* Number 44, May 1970.

Bontwell, W. D. "Our Leisure-time Education," *Education Digest,* Number 35, December 1969.

Divoky, D. "Underground or Independent High School Press," *Catholic School Journal,* February 1970.

Dumas, Wayne, and Beckner Weldon. *Introduction to Secondary Education: A Foundations Approach,* Scranton, PA: International Textbook Company, 1968.

Frederick, Robert W. *Student Activities in American Education,* New York: The Center for Applied Research in Education, 1965.

Frederick, Robert W. *The Third Curriculum,* New York: Appleton Century-Crofts, 1959.

Grahan, Grace. "Improving Student Participation," Washington, D.C.: *National Association of Secondary School Principals Bulletin,* 1966.

Hearn, Arthur C. "Evaluation of Student Activities," Washington, D.C.: *National Association of Secondary School Principals Bulletin,* 1966.

McGuire, R. C. "Help Your Student Council Justify Its Existence," *Journal of Secondary Education,* Number 45, April 1970.

Postlethvaite, T. N. *School Organization and Student Achievement,* New York: John Wiley and Sons, Inc., 1967.

Robbins, Jerry H., B. Stirling, and S. William. *Student Activities in the Innovative School,* Minneapolis: Burgess Publishing Company, 1969.

Stroup, Herbert. *Toward a Philosophy of Organized Student Activities,* Minneapolis: University of Minnesota Press, 1964.

Sullivan, R. J. "Overrated Threat: What to do about Underground Newspapers," *National Association of Secondary School Principals Bulletin,* Number 53, September 1969.

Chapter 7
Innovation and Change

Today's administrators are being bombarded constantly by innovations for all educational levels. Programs to upgrade science education, minicourses, state accountability plans, open classrooms, and a multitude of other ideas initiated by teachers, interest groups, and reformers reach administrators' desks. As time passes, the number of changes expands constantly.

A major factor in initiating, planning, effecting, and evaluating changes in local school districts is the administration. In the school district, the superintendent is the crucial officer; in individual schools, the principal is the key man.

With his power to allocate personnel, money, and time, the superintendent can encourage or stifle change. He may be the chief cause for the continuation of status quo.

At the local building level, the principal also creates a climate. He may encourage or discourage innovation. On a more limited level, he handles available resources which may be earmarked for changes. As the key person, he may provide or deny support of new ideas. When he is sympathetic, the probable success of a proposed change is enhanced. If he is unaware or hostile, his attitude usually throttles innovation.

Change occurs in many ways. It may develop naturally and create no hostility. It may be planned or unplanned, simple or complex. It may have specific goals or be aimless. It may be a positive or negative change.

The school administrator should examine with infinite pain new proposals in a local school or school district. He must evaluate the pros and cons of the new concept, and he must assure himself that the plan meets the needs of students, faculty, parents, the school district, and the state.

As he works with teachers, the administrator will develop skill in identifying and eliminating the factors which inhibit change. With experience, he will further his skill in developing those factors that are conducive to change.

Fly in the Ointment

The language arts/social studies group, an interdisciplinary team from Cope Middle School, had scheduled its bi-weekly planning meeting for 3:15. Mr. Howe and Mrs. Stearns, social studies teachers, arrived ten minutes early.

"Mr. Cary and Mrs. Stall couldn't be here today," Mr. Howe announced. But Mr. Cesarz, our glorious team leader, should arrive soon. Would you like to glance at the unipac I've finished for our unit on prejudice?"

Mrs. Stearns looked at the unipac. "Wow, this is really relevant stuff. It's neat the way this value exercise lets the kids consider their feelings toward minorities."

"I'll buy that," Mr. Howe replied. "But I'm worried. If this unipac *really* is to work, we all must use the values techniques with the students. I'm not sure everyone will approve of this values stuff. It's too bad we can't have their cooperation and input. After all we're supposed to be a team . . ."

"Right on," Mrs. Stearns nodded. "Well, you've done your job. It's up to the rest of us to help implement this unipac."

"You know," Mr. Howe mused aloud, "I worked so hard on this thing because your students were super in role-playing activities last week. They're still talking about the skits you used in your communism unit. I hate to say it, but Mrs. Stall's students were disappointed. You know she lectured rather than participate in role-playing. I really wanted to talk about this student feedback today."

She shrugged. "It's too bad that the teachers who'd profit aren't here," said Mrs. Stearns. "Hi, Mr. Cesarz."

Mr. Cesarz looked tired. He sat down wearily. "Please forgive my tardiness."

Mr. Howe showed the unipac to Mr. Cesarz. "Hey," he said, "Is this dynamite! Boy, I'd love to try this with my kids."

They kicked around some ideas and suggestions for using the unipac. At last Mrs. Stearns asked: "Do you think Mr. Cary will do the Value Island Game?"

"Perhaps he can be the roving tutor during this unit."

"Well," Mr. Howe interrupted. "He's never supported the team effort. You know how he feels about values. He's traditional all the way. It's textbook and tough discipline."

Mrs. Stearns sighed. "He's always complaining about the informality in my classes. He doesn't like class discussions. He seems even to resent the students' desire to be in my classes."

"Let's be honest," said Mr. Cesarz. "The principal pushed this team effort. We've given it the old college try. It's almost impossible to work together if our beliefs about learning and students are so different. How can we work together? I'm really sick and tired of beating my head against the administrative wall."

DISCUSSION QUESTIONS

1. What are several pros and cons of team teaching as discussed in this case study?
2. Is there a more suitable team structure that could enhance communication among team members?
3. How could a principal improve the functioning of this team?
4. How open should team members be when communicating with each other?
5. Should team members have similar beliefs regarding learning and students?
6. Should negative feedback from students be shared with teachers? Explain your response.
7. Is value clarification a proper topic in a middle school classroom?

Bookish Parents

Mrs. Hansen, a social studies teacher in a modern California high school, instigated a new program based on the inquiry approach. She decided to utilize newspapers, textbooks, supplementary books, and various special topic pamphlets. They were to be available during class. The library promised to carry on reserve duplicates of her materials.

Many of the assignments and readings were dependent on the special topic pamphlets. Students complained, however, that they couldn't obtain the materials. Since the readings were so crucial, students were handicapped. Some students inquired about buying copies, and Mrs. Hansen expedited their purchases.

As semester grades were being recorded, four parents arrived at school and complained about the pamphlet problem. One parent asserted, "It's up to you, Mrs. Hansen, to provide the same materials for all students. It's not fair otherwise." Another said, "I never had to buy my books when I was in school. Why can't you use just one text?" "No one told me about this purchasing scheme," a mother said. "My budget can't stand another $5.00 for books. I have three other children to consider." "Are the students who purchased the books getting the highest grades?"

Mrs. Hansen was red-faced. "I didn't realize there was any problem. I've tried to help all students and even allowed them to study in teams. The students don't seem to be upset."

Then a spokeswoman of the group stated: "We've decided to go to the board of education and ask them to purchase enough books for every student in class. No child should be penalized for not having a book."

DISCUSSION QUESTIONS

1. What could you suggest to Mrs. Hansen as a possible solution to this problem?
2. What role should the building principal play in this parent-teacher conference?
3. Should multiple sources of information be used in a class?
4. What factors must be considered before instituting a new course in the curriculum?
5. How could Mrs. Hansen increase the communication level between student and teacher in her class?
6. Why did Mrs. Hansen get upset and defensive over the textbook situation?

Being Different at Einstein High

As the new member of Einstein High School math department, Marg Densmore had been assigned the general math classes. Realizing that these students were not the school's "brightest," she designed a course

Innovation and Change

which stressed math survival skills. She stated course goals and objectives, used practical math problems, and utilized an evaluation system which was criterion-referenced. Many students were excited about math for the first time in their schooling. Their mathematics skills applied to real life problems.

"Miss Densmore, I like math this year," one student admitted, and another chimed in with, "Me too! Our ratio problems help me in my work at the grocery store."

At the end of the first grading period, Marg averaged the grades. She gave the following: A-6, B-10, C-8, D-2, E-0.

Two days later the principal called Marg into his office.

"Marg, I like your enthusiasm and ideas in the general math class. But your grades are too high," said Mr. Daus. "Everyone knows you're working with the bottom level students. Normally they don't get A's and B's. How do you think the algebra and geometry classes feel about your students receiving high grades?"

"Mr. Daus," she replied, "I've stated my course objectives. You approved them. I can show that my students accomplished them, and with high levels of competence."

"That may well be true, but we must establish limits for low level classes. I'm afraid I must ask you to revise your program or your marking system so that the students receive lower grades. This will be compatible with the philosophy of the math department."

DISCUSSION QUESTIONS

1. Was Marg's position a valid one and should she have argued more strenuously?
2. Does the principal have the right to require a teacher to change his teaching style and grading system?
3. Would you suggest that Marg grieve this procedure, talk to other department members, or make a visit to the superintendent?
4. What suggestions can you offer a new teacher for instituting new courses and class procedures?
5. Should school districts "label" students by tracking them into classes that are designed to give low grades?

The Boss Blows It

For six months Mr. Ray, the curriculum coordinator, had worked with a special career education committee to design a K-12 career education program for the Mt. Hood School District. Committee members were enthusiastic about the community involvement in the project.

At a meeting one evening, Mr. Jones, a committee member, was addressing the group about the time Mr. Shockley, the superintendent, walked in. "The career awareness phase of our program is arranged," Mr. Jones was saying. "The K-6 students may opt to participate in a local business, or they may invite different community resource people to talk to their classes."

Mr. Ackerman, another committee member, added, "Perhaps we can name a district placement coordinator who will help students find different jobs to give them a feel for a career."

After thirty minutes of listening, Mr. Shockley spoke up. "I hope you folks aren't taking this program for granted. It seems to me you're getting involved in things that don't concern you. I don't favor turning students loose on the community. And anyway, our local businessmen can't take time from their work to speak to our classes. What we need — and the board recently brought this to my attention — is a K-12 textbook series on career education. This committee might review the various series and recommend one to the board. I wonder if next month you might put your recommendation on my desk so that we can adopt the program. That will be a fine contribution to the education of students in our district."

"Meeting adjourned," announced Mr. Ray, the curriculum coordinator.

DISCUSSION QUESTIONS

1. What alternate strategies for change could the curriculum coordinator have used instead of the one mentioned above?
2. What could the curriculum coordinator do to re-establish the enthusiasm of the committee?
3. What should the superintendent's role be in matters of curriculum change and innovation?
4. Should the superintendent be involved as a member of the curriculum committee?
5. Was the superintendent considerate of the feelings of the curriculum coordinator?

Innovation and Change

A Dangerous Precedent

Thurston Elementary School principal, Jerry Waverly, was concerned about moving into a new open-space school in September. Although his teachers had offered token suggestions to the architect on instructional needs, none had been consulted in regard to the operations of the open classroom.

Jerry called on the superintendent, Mr. Clyde Openheimer.

"Clyde," Jerry began, "I'm concerned about my teaching staff. They have to have time to plan the new curriculum for next year in the new building."

Mr. Openheimer leaned back in his chair. "Look, Jerry, the teachers' contract calls for two in-service days. You've already used them. We can't afford special bus runs this late in the year."

"I understand this is a late request, but it's expecting too much of a group of teachers accustomed to traditional classrooms to be thrust into large open space areas that demand team planning and teaching — don't you think so?"

The superintendent pondered a moment. "I guess I think if a person is an effective teacher in a self-contained classroom, he'll do as well in an open classroom. I know how conscientious you are, Jerry, but you worry too much. Buy some resource books, bring in a speaker for an after-school faculty meeting, and everything will work out."

"Mr. Openheimer," exclaimed Jerry, "You miss my point. The new building is a real threat to our teachers and the new program which it demands. Buying books or meeting for an hour — well, it won't help the teachers. Could you find some money to pay their salaries for two weeks this summer? We'll meet together and really detail plans for the new program in the new school."

The superintendent laughed congenially. "You know, Jerry, you're a young and energetic administrator. You haven't learned to see the potential ramifications of your proposal. If I pay your teachers for this summer project, I'd be obligated to pay teachers in other buildings to develop similar programs. A precedent like that is potentially dangerous. I know you'll figure something out."

Critical Incidents In School Administration

DISCUSSION QUESTIONS

1. What are some ways that in-service education can be built into a school calendar?
2. Could Mr. Openheimer have been more supportive of Mr. Waverly's proposal? In what ways?
3. Do you believe in the phrase "Form Follows Function" with regard to a new building and program?
4. To what extent should teachers be involved in developing new buildings and programs?
5. What alternatives did Mr. Waverly have after the denial of the superintendent for in-service money to prepare teachers?

Blind Flight

During the fall orientation meetings for beginning teachers, the principal, Mrs. Goodenough, explained her open-door policy. "Whenever you have a problem, bring it to the office." Dennis took her at her word and made an appointment to talk about his first month of teaching.

After warm greetings, Dennis said, "It's being a wonderful experience. The students are wonderful, and I'm more than enthusiastic about my biology classes. I'm having trouble with history. You recall it was my minor. I need to prepare every night just to keep ahead of the students. It's real tough making lesson plans and finding materials to motivate the students."

"Years ago when I began teaching, I had similar problems." Then she added, "Did I ever tell you about that walleye I caught last year? It was the biggest fish taken out of Ranger Lake all summer! I'll tell you, Dennis, you've got to work hard on your planning. You might ask some experienced teachers for help."

From then on several veteran teachers constantly asked Dennis if he was having troubles in the classroom. At last Dennis queried them: "Why are you asking me all those questions?" They all replied that the principal had asked them to "look after" and "help" Dennis.

After the principal visited and evaluated Dennis, he received a report which stated that he was improving in his lesson planning and locating instructional materials for class.

Innovation and Change

DISCUSSION QUESTIONS

1. Why should a principal keep personal conversations confidential?
2. What does a beginning teacher risk by sharing problems and frustrations with an administrator?
3. What rights does a teacher have in challenging an administrator's evaluation report?
4. What role should the principal play when working with beginning teachers?
5. Should veteran teachers evaluate beginning teachers?

Bandwagons and Change

During the summer Mr. Bandwagon, the principal of Freedom Middle School, attended a conference on flexible scheduling and team teaching. He saw a number of implications and uses for these innovations in the middle school.

At the fall orientation meeting before school opened, he made what came to be known as his "famous speech." "Colleagues, the time has come. We have a chance to make learning far more exciting and beneficial to our students. For years we have believed that our students must have six subjects a day with one teacher responsible for each subject. I've drawn up a new plan. It involves a schedule of sixteen modules per day with each of you operating as a member of a team. The students will have curricular options, and we'll adjust our class time to fit our objectives. We have five days before school begins to plan. Since you have no questions, let's get to work. I've briefed the team leaders, and they'll fill in the details. Good luck, gang!"

"Who does he think he is? Don't we have a voice in the matter?" asked one teacher.

"I'll grieve this thing," said another.

"Doesn't the curriculum committee count for something or did the committee become the team leaders?"

"I can't work with Mrs. Giles now! How can I function with her as a team member?

"Let's get a petition and fight this thing!"

> **DISCUSSION QUESTIONS**
> 1. What are the different procedures for effecting curricular change?
> 2. What might the principal have done to prepare his staff for change?
> 3. What options does the staff have in opposing such changes?
> 4. In your teaching experience, can you think of any changes that resulted from administrators jumping on the latest bandwagon?

Beware of Jealousy

During the spring, three of Tempe High School's finest teachers brought a pilot project proposal to Mr. Douglas, the principal.

Jerry White, the science teacher, was the spokesman. "We — Martha, Sid, and I — want to team-teach English, social studies, and science. We'd like to take the old cafeteria and remodel it so it would have a capacity of 100 students. We've sketched out our plans. There would be independent study carrels, small group areas, and a large lecture-lab arrangement. We'll donate our time this summer. All we ask is that the school supply the paint. We're all 'sold' on the interdisciplinary approach to learning because we believe it will help the students see the interrelationships of subjects. Here's a sample of our first unit. We think it'll be a grand project."

The principal beamed. "This is wonderful. Your preparation, enthusiasm, and commitment are exemplary. I'll be most happy to support this kind of undertaking. The cafeteria isn't going to be used next year anyway. So there's no reason why we can't proceed tentatively until we get the approval of the superintendent and board of education."

All that week, the teachers' lounge was filled with rumors and rancor. "Jerry White's angling for the assistant principal's job next year." "Those young whippersnappers will let the kids get away with everything and anything." "The noise will drive us right up the wall." "Old man Douglas always favors the young teachers. Why he wouldn't even buy the materials I asked for three months ago."

Can't you see the excitement in the student's faces?

Critical Incidents In School Administration

> **DISCUSSION QUESTIONS**
> 1. What are the administrative problems of sanctioning a pilot project involving a few faculty members?
> 2. How can an administrator support individual and small group requests for change without alienating the remainder of the staff?
> 3. Could you suggest a procedure which a teacher or a team of teachers might use to effect change in a school?
> 4. What other considerations must be involved in granting a request such as the one described in this case study?

A Directive from the Superintendent

At the summer district administrator's retreat, Superintendent Porter sent a directive to all principals stating that every teacher in their buildings must develop a set of performance objectives for each class they taught. These objectives were to be submitted one month after school's opening. Mr. Porter announced he had hired an outside consultant to help the staff write objectives on the opening in-service day of orientation work.

In view of the superintendent's order, Mr. Weigand, principal of Earsworth Elementary School, sent to his teachers on the first day this note: "Friends, Superintendent Porter has asked me to inform you that written performance objectives for your courses must be handed in one month from today. This afternoon at the in-service meeting you will receive instruction in composing these objectives."

In a discussion, one teacher asked, "Is anything wrong with our teaching? Is this the reason we have to spend hours writing objectives?"

"I don't think that's the case. Probably he's getting pressure from the state department."

"Well," said a second teacher, "I can't see how all this business will improve my classroom. In fact, because of the time it'll take me to write objectives, it may hurt my teaching. I should be working on lesson plans."

"I was told to inform all of you to write performance objectives. If you want to talk about it, call Mr. Porter. Any more questions. . .?"

Innovation and Change

DISCUSSION QUESTIONS

1. What role should the principal play in carrying out a directive from the superintendent?
2. What voice should teachers have in carrying out a change such as this one?
3. Is it fair to ask teachers to do this work in addition to other teaching duties?
4. Can you think of other positive benefits that might justify this activity?
5. Is an administrative decree the best means of effecting change and innovation?
6. How can the principal encourage change in a more humane manner than a directive from the superintendent?

Female Curmudgeon

Miss Feutz, in her honors English class, purposely created an informal atmosphere. She believed that her students would improve in their ability to interact under conditions that were relaxing and unthreatening. Classes began with a warm-up designed to involve students with each other, and the exercise led to a discussion of the day's reading assignment.

One afternoon in November, the principal, Miss Dove, arrived before the class had convened and announced she would be evaluating Miss Feutz today.

"May I visit you today?" asked Miss Dove.

"Of course. Any time," Miss Feutz replied with confidence.

The students streamed in as usual. There was laughter and loud talk while they went to their seats in the circle. Obviously they enjoyed this open, rather free time in coming to order.

"Okay, class, we have a visitor today. Let's see if we can make Miss Dove feel as if she's a part of the class," began Miss Feutz. She looked at Jim. "You're responsible for the warm-up today. Would you begin please?"

Jim was a highly creative student. After explaining the warm-up to the class, he distributed a blank card to each person. Then he issued directions. "First, put your name in the center. In the upper right hand corner, write three words ending in - *ing* which describe you. In the bottom right hand corner, list the title of a book you read recently which really turned you on. In the upper left hand corner, describe yourself in three adjectives, and in the bottom left corner, write a sentence describing the school."

When the writing was completed, he concluded: "Now with the Scotch tape, fasten your card on yourself and we'll walk around and see what you've written."

The classroom buzzed conversation, occasional laughter, and, "Oh, look at this!" When the five minutes of sharing and interacting ended, the principal had disappeared.

After school, Miss Feutz was called into the principal's office. "As you know, I visited your room this morning," Miss Dove began. "I'm quite troubled. I thought I'd hear a high level discussion or lecture on English literature. Instead it was chaos and noise. There was no lesson plan. You are teaching our best young people, honor students. We have a duty to prepare them for college. I see no reason to waste time with fun and games."

"Miss Dove, I was disappointed that you left so soon. We had a fine discussion of *Hamlet*. Then the students did Hamlet's death scene. It was superb and my students are learning to share facts, feelings, and values. The group is closely knit and learns. You observed a warm-up exercise. The design helps to reinforce our feelings and allows us to accomplish much more at the fact and concept level."

"There is a time and a place for everything," Miss Dove stated coldly. "I never can accept this kind of activity in the classroom. I hope when I visit you again in a few weeks there will be considerable improvement."

DISCUSSION QUESTIONS
1. How does an administrator who subscribes to a particular teaching philosophy support a teacher who holds a different philosophy?
2. Can you suggest another procedure which Miss Dove could have used in her evaluation process?
3. What would you suggest to a teacher who wants to use teaching methods which might be unacceptable to a building principal?
4. How can an administrator establish a climate of support and trust with a teaching staff?

STUDENT REACTION SHEET

INSTRUCTOR _____ STUDENT _____

COURSE _____ DATE _____

CRITICAL INCIDENT _____

REACTION:

_____
_____
_____
_____
_____
_____
_____
_____
_____
_____
_____
_____
_____
_____
_____
_____

REFERENCES CITED

1. _____
2. _____
3. _____
4. _____

SELECTED REFERENCES
INNOVATION AND CHANGE

"Alternative Schools: Symposium," *Phi Delta Kappan,* Number 54, March 1973.

Cereghino, E. "Innovations Without Added Cost," *Clearinghouse,* Number 48, March 1974.

"Colloquy on Educational Reform," *National Elementary Principal's Bulletin,* Number 52, April 1974.

Crowin, R.G. "Innovations in Organizations," *Sociology of Education,* Number 48, Winter 1975.

Eurich, Alvin. *High School 1980,* New York: Pitman Publishing Corporation, 1970.

Haden, Herbert and Jean King. *Educational Innovator's Guide,* Worthington, Ohio: Jones Press, 1974.

Helsel, A.R. "Teacher's Acceptance of Innovation and Innovation Characteristics," *High School Journal,* Number 56, November 1972.

Hull, W.L. "Installing Innovations Via Inservice Education," *Theory Into Practice,* Number 4, February 1975.

Kline, L.W. "Perils of Innovation," *Reading Teacher,* Number 28, October 1974.

Nasca, Donald. "Open Education: Is It For You?," *Instructor,* Number 83, October 1973.

Parsons, Cynthia. *Schools Can Change,* Boston: Sterling Institute Press, 1969.

Schwadron, Abraham. "Are We Ready for Aesthetic Education?," *Music Educators Journal,* Number 60, October 1973.

Shane, H.G. "Innovation: An Ongoing Process Symposium," *Educational Leadership,* Number 30, March 1973.

Smith, Vernon. "Alternative Public Schools: What Are They," *National Association of Secondary School Principal's Bulletin,* Number 54, September 1973.

Sullivan, P.E. "Principal As Good Guy," *National Association of Secondary School Principal's Bulletin,* Number 58, December 1974.

Toepfer, C.F. "Supervisor's Responsibility for Innovation," *Educational Leadership,* Number 30, May 1973.

Unruh, Glenys and Robert Leeper. *Influences in Curriculum Change,* Washington, D.C.: Association for Supervision and Curriculum Development, 1968.

Chapter 8

Support Services

Although frequently hidden from the public eye, the special services personnel enable the administrative and instructional staff of a school district to operate with greater ease and efficiency. The custodians, bus drivers, contractors, mechanics, secretaries, crossing guards, cooks, and counselors all may expedite the smooth operation of a school program.

The dictionary definition of support is "to hold up or in position, to maintain, to uphold one by aid or countenance." It is a fitting explanation. Often overlooked in their importance in behind-the-scenes work, the support services personnel add to and supplement the regular school program and staff. Since in most schools these people remain in the background, they are noticed only when they make mistakes.

Support services fall into two categories. First are those which are peripherally related to the instructional program (school counselors, reading specialists, social workers, psychometrists, speech therapists, and others). Second are those who are associated with health, safety, maintenance services (custodians, cooks, bus drivers, groundsmen, secretaries, and others).

The first group devotes the majority of time to students and their families; the second group focuses on things.

It is a contemporary truism that specially trained personnel are essential to the child's *whole* development. Recognizing that the emotional and learning growth are interrelated, educators are responsible for the variety and number of counselors and social workers in our schools. Many taxpayers feel, however, support services of a professional nature should come from the classroom teacher. In a complex and diverse culture, students are beset by all kinds of problems which demand professional help. Although the teacher is a specialist in his area, he cannot serve as a

Critical Incidents In School Administration

"be all" for his students. Thus, if one believes that education aims for development of the whole person, support services assume great significance. As years pass, they seem destined to become even more important in the schools.

Support services must remain just that. In their contribution to optimum educational results, special services must not usurp nor undercut the role of the instructional staff. The school administrator's job is to help establish a symbiotic relationship between teachers and the support services personnel.

Union Muscle

The newspaper story read as follows:

> The Marygrove School District Board of Education, at its last night's meeting, accepted the low bids from the following contractors for construction of the new Wright Elementary School: Mechanical Contract — Mason and Sons; Electrical Contract — Newman Bros.; General Contract — Hollinson.

The fact was generally known that Hollinson was an independent, non-union company and that the other two were unionized. It was no surprise a day or two later to observe fifty pickets outside the board of education building. They objected to the use of the non-union general contractor. Superintendent Dr. Sam Mason received several phone calls from community leaders who protested the use of a non-union firm. Dr. Mason called a special open meeting of the board of education. Among the many citizens who came, a number of placards and picket signs were held high, and some men and women spoke against the Hollinson Building Company.

The president of the Marygrove Chamber of Commerce, John Parr, spoke out for the community: "Ladies and gentlemen of the board, you know we're a labor town. As a result, a considerable number of the townspeople protest the board action of a contract to a non-unionized firm. In addition, Hollinson has a history of substandard building, the result at least in part caused by his use of non-union men. This school district must build new buildings in the best interests of the community. Our taxpayers owe their livelihood and their loyalty to union shops. It seems tactless and not in their interests to turn to non-union people."

"You also know that Hollinson's firm has been picketed, their trucks and equipment vandalized, and their men beaten up. Here in Marygrove we don't want that to occur. I have here for the board a petition signed by 5,000 residents who protest the hiring of Hollinson Builders."

> **DISCUSSION QUESTIONS**
>
> 1. How should the board of education respond to the petition signed by 5,000 Marygrove residents?
> 2. What options does the board of education have, if it truly wishes to award the general contract to another builder?
> 3. What are the steps a board of education should take in awarding bids to contractors?
> 4. As superintendent of schools, how would you react to the report by the president of the chamber of commerce?

She Breathed Fire

For six years Mrs. Bea McKinstry drove a school bus for the Paradise Hills School District. She was an excellent driver with an accident-free record and a reputation for being gentle and considerate of the pupils who rode in her bus. During the current semester, she attended every board meeting and spoke out against several of the board's transportation policies and curricular suggestions. Many board members were irate over her questions and her citing research to confirm her ideas about curriculum. Finally she organized a citizens' group who attended board meetings and raised embarrassing questions about policy.

On March 12, the superintendent called Mrs. McKinstry to his office. When she arrived, he said with vigor, "I must inform you that next year you will not be hired as a bus driver. Several reports from the head mechanic indicate that you have not followed procedures for cleaning your bus. In addition, all the other bus drivers have sent me a petition. They have requested you be removed as a driver next year. My only recourse — I'm sorry to say — is to ask for your resignation in writing."

Mrs. McKinstry got angry. "I'm not-a-going to resign, and don't you forget it. The charges against me are absurd. What you're doing is penalizing me — you and the board — for my political activities and my criticism of the board. I want you to tell the board that I'm a citizen in this community, and I have three children in the schools. In short, I'm not only a bus driver. I'm a tax payer and a parent. And I have every right to express my opinions. Go back to the dimwits on the board and tell them I won't quit. And if they fire me, I'll go to court. Put that in your pipe and smoke it."

> **DISCUSSION QUESTIONS**
> 1. What legal recourse does Mrs. McKinstry have to fight her case?
> 2. What role should the support staff play in school district policies and procedures?
> 3. As superintendent, what action would you have taken in the Bea McKinstry case?
> 4. Through what channels should staff members, support or instructional, be allowed to voice their opinions?

Object Lesson

Mrs. Denise Greyhound, a veteran bus driver, prided herself on being a stern disciplinarian. At the beginning of the school year, she distributed a printed list of rules and regulations to the riders, and she enforced them to the letter of the law. As a rule, few behavior problems developed. On November 3, a situation arose. She decided to initiate an object-lesson.

When she picked up her bus riders after school, she noticed on the tarmac the fifth grade bully, Brian Young, trying to fight with John Ridell and Norman Braun, also fifth graders.

"Brian Young," she screamed, "If you want to ride home on this bus, stop your bullying. I won't stand for this behavior!"

When the fifth graders boarded the bus, the incident continued. Brian shot paper wads at John and Norman. They called him a big mouth. When other students got involved, the driver stopped the bus at the side of the road.

Rising from her seat, she faced the children and said, "It looks to me that you riders have forgotten the rules of good behavior on this bus. I can't drive safely with all the noise and confusion on the bus. Since I can't trust you to obey the rules, I'm going to teach you a lesson. We're going back to the bus garage and we're going to sit there until you are quiet. I'm not fooling, believe me."

The bus remained at the bus garage for forty-five minutes. At last she started the bus run.

Support Services

Since the bus was so very late, the superintendent and principal were besieged with phone calls from anxious parents who wanted to know the whereabouts of their children. Unfortunately, Mrs. Greyhound had not informed the principal or superintendent of her therapy. As a result, the administrators were as much in the dark as the parents.

DISCUSSION QUESTIONS

1. Evaluate Mrs. Greyhound's method for dealing with misbehavior on the bus, and discuss other options she might have selected.
2. Should the superintendent react to Mrs. Greyhound's behavior as a bus driver?
3. Should school bus drivers maintain common behavior policies for student riders?
4. Can you suggest activities to be included in school bus drivers' training sessions?

A Wet Problem

The Youngstown School District, constructing a multi-million dollar school, had hired Frank Plight and Associates as its architect. Research and planning had included staff and community involvement. Everyone was thrilled about moving into the new school building.

On a bright spring morning, as Mr. Morley Weber, a veteran superintendent, made his daily round of the new building, he noticed a peculiar situation with the building's foundation. He immediately called Mr. Plight, the architect, to meet him as soon as possible.

At 4:00 p.m. Mr. Weber told the architect that the building seemed to be two feet below grade level.

"We know what we're doing. You tend school. We'll do the building. There's nothing to worry about. I've studied the building specs. I can vouch for the fact that the building is properly located. If you're worried about drainage problems, forget it. We've put in sewers to handle water. Anyway, I'm paid to worry about such things. Let's get a cup of coffee and discuss our next building program."

Mr. Weber sighed with relief. "I must admit that when I saw the building this morning, I had visions of water draining into the school and

"Mr. Plight, it appears to me that this building is sitting two feet below grade level."

ruining the new carpets and furniture. I'm glad I don't have to worry. I got enough other stuff to worry about."

Six months later the school district forked over $250,000 to install a sump pump system. Water simply flooded the new school building. Ironically, there was proof positive that the building had been built two feet below grade level!

DISCUSSION QUESTIONS

1. What role should the superintendent play in working with an architect?
2. What responsibilities does the architect have in building a new school building?
3. Does the Youngstown School District have any grounds for suing the architect or contractor in this case?

---

10 % Budget; 90 % Bitching

Ivan Palmer had been the head bus mechanic for twenty years in the Libertyville School District. An expert mechanic, he kept the vehicles running year in and year out in spite of many personnel, time, and financial problems. His great sense of timing and his inveterate honesty proved both strengths and weaknesses.

In early spring, Ivan was in the midst of a hectic week. Three buses were in the shop for repairs. Necessary spare parts had not arrived from the company. Since the district maintained only three spare buses, Ivan desperately needed the parts.

Mr. Warren Zuehls, assistant superintendent of transportation, phoned Ivan. "Number 58 is stalled on Pioneer Road. It's got to be towed in. Can you drive a spare bus out there and switch buses so that we can get the kids home?"

"Gosh, Mr. Zuehls, I don't have a spare bus. The damn parts haven't come in. So three buses just aren't operable. When the first bus gets back, I'll go pick up the kids."

"You mean you haven't repaired those buses yet? They've been out of kilter for over a week now. Seems to me you could have made some parts yourself to get us by. Anyway, we're spending too much money and time on repairs. Tell me: how can three buses break down at the same time?"

"Mr. Zuehls, with all due respect to you, sir, your last statements bother me. Twenty years ago I never had problems with bus repairs. Then the district operated a total of ten buses. Now we got fifty. I've got two arms and two legs. I can't do all the shopwork on that many buses. In the bargain, I work with 10 per cent of the budget and 90 per cent of the bitching. It don't make sense."

DISCUSSION QUESTIONS

1. What is the main issue in this case study?
2. How much authority should the head mechanic have in operating a school bus garage?
3. In this case, suggest several ways to improve the Libertyville School District's transportation operation.

Bossy Flossy

Flossy Moran, the principal's secretary at Fields Middle School, prided herself on running a tight ship. As the secretary at Fields for ten years, she knew the policies and procedures of school operation. She had helped the principal develop procedures for use of supplies and AV equipment, and had designed various forms for attendance and lunch count. In addition, she oversaw these activities and had developed procedures for student, parent, and teacher requests. Each time someone entered the principal's office, Flossy was equal to the occasion. She asked their business and promptly helped them finish it.

One day Mr. Crabtree, the new language arts teacher, asked to see the principal about a field trip.

"Oh, you can't go on a field trip! It's too late in the year. All field trip requests must be in by the end of April. This is May 5."

"You can't be serious," chuckled Mr. Crabtree. "The father of a student in my class owns McDonalds. He has invited us to tour the business and have lunch 'on the house.' It's a great supplement to the unit on career education. Besides, it'll be a great experience for my students. Don't you think the principal would make an exception?"

She drew herself up and shrugged, "If we make your field trip an exception, every other teacher must be allowed to go too. We have a policy. It's the same for everyone. Maybe you can take your class to

McDonald's after school some afternoon. Anything else I can do for you?" asked Flossy. She turned back to some papers on her desk.

Recognizing her rudeness, he sauntered into the hall. He wondered if he should talk to the principal. After all, the trip had a powerful educational benefit for his students. He was also rankled by the secretary's telling him what he could and could not do. Subconsciously he thought of Mrs. Moran as "Bossy Flossy."

DISCUSSION QUESTIONS

1. How do you feel about a principal's secretary making decisions like Flossy did?
2. Explain the cliche, "The secretary is the person who really runs the school."
3. As a principal, what responsibilities would you deem appropriate for your secretary?

No Business of Hers

The East Bend School District hired Miss Shirley Dogood, a school social worker. Her job was to help the people in this depressed community to improve their mental and physical health. The new employee was a young energetic person. She had initiated a breakfast program at school, a Tiny Tot Story Hour, and a neighborhood clinic for physical and mental health. She also had made numerous home visits in her work with parents. Mid-year, Shirley began her follow-up program and decided to observe in the classroom some of the children whose parents she worked with.

For one month she visited classrooms. Then she made an appointment to talk with Jerry Wise, the superintendent.

"I'm delighted to meet you at last." Mr. Wise was somewhat embarrassed that he hadn't met Shirley earlier. "We were fortunate to have this position created for us by special federal funds. I'm hopeful for fine results from your work with the school and community."

"Thank you, Mr. Wise," Miss Dogood replied. She had not expected such a warm welcome, but she quickly regained her composure.

"You know I've lived and worked in this community for seven months. I believe the lives of hundreds of people in this community have been brightened. Of late, I've visited the classes of the students in my case load. I don't like to be critical, Mr. Wise, but I was appalled at the classroom behavior of the teachers. They seldom accepted feelings of students, and they neither praised nor encouraged student talk. Classrooms, in my opinion, were dull, sterile, cold, and unexcited."

Then she added, "I'd like to suggest that the district plan and implement a teacher in-service program devoted to humanizing classrooms. I know a university professor who'd gladly help us with the program."

Superintendent Wise reacted grimly. "Miss Dogood, I appreciate your work as a social worker and your interest in this district. But I feel I must say it is not in your province to comment on classroom climate and learning. That's the principal's job. If you wish to speak with individual teachers about the special needs of the students in your caseload, that's likely to be helpful."

DISCUSSION QUESTIONS

1. Did Miss Dogood act professionally in sharing her observations about the classrooms with Superintendent Wise?
2. What should be the role of a school social worker?
3. Can you suggest a means by which special service people can aid the classroom teachers?

CIA in Levenworth

Levenworth School District was in a small rural area and had excellent relationships with the local police force. In fact, during the summer months, Ed Broski, middle school vice-principal, was a volunteer police officer. Of late, the community had suffered a rash of home robberies. Despite all efforts, the police had no leads.

Mr. Broski's school work gave him access to a valid rumor grapevine. One day he heard that a small group of middle school boys were bragging about having bought new watches and stereo equipment.

Next morning Mr. Broski told the police chief that some information about possible suspects might be available if he dropped by the school. In ten minutes, Chief Bucky Walters knocked on Mr. Broski's door.

"Hi, Chief. Sit down. I'm glad you stopped over. I might have some clues. Now I'm not positive about the involvement of our kids in the robberies, but they're sporting new watches, and the grapevine mentions stereos and small TV's. Some of the boys have been known to get into trouble before." He listed several names.

"Yeah, now that you mention them," the chief said, "You may be on the right track. Two of those guys have been in trouble with the law before. Both have spent time at the juvenile home. Let's go look in their lockers. Maybe we'll turn up something. If we find serial numbers on any equipment, that'll help. If we draw a blank, we'll talk to each boy privately, you know, just to shake them up."

Mr. Broski paused, "Let's wait until the classes change before we go into the halls. I don't want to tip the boys off."

DISCUSSION QUESTIONS

1. Was Vice-principal Broski correct in calling Police Chief Walters in the robbery case?
2. What are the students' rights in situations such as the one described in this case study?
3. What are other situations which warrant calling the police for help in school?
4. Will the students' rights be violated by a locker search?

Wasted Motion

Dr. Mario Wickman, Superintendent of the Woodstock Public School District, knew that if a new elementary school building were built, he would need strong public support. Since the PTA was a representative group, he suggested the members form a Citizen's Committee to gather information on various open elementary school buildings and programs. The parents were delighted. They really wanted to help and were excited about a new open-concept school.

Mrs. Jerome Cazett, PTA President, organized the parents and devised a plan of study. Ten parents met regularly and shared information from books, articles, and visits with local teachers and administrators. In addition, the members visited open elementary schools all over the state. One parent paid her own fare to attend a conference on the subject.

Six months later, Mrs. Cazett and her committee presented their findings and recommendations to the superintendent.

"We appreciate your meeting with us this evening," said Mrs. Cazett. "We've gathered a great deal of information and have recommendations for you."

For some time the committee conversed with the superintendent. He seemed greatly interested. At the completion of the presentation, Dr. Wickman shocked the committee — and community — by saying: "After studying the possibilities for a new open elementary school, I've concluded we really do not need the open-concept school. Instead, the future of the schools lies in a reorganized curriculum based on individualized instruction. That means we will have to add only four classrooms to our already existing building."

DISCUSSION QUESTIONS

1. What effects do you think Dr. Wickman's statement had on the Citizen's Committee?
2. For what purposes should a Citizen's Committee be utilized by a school district?
3. What should be the composition of a Citizen's Committee?
4. Even if Dr. Wickman had an alternative plan, how should he have reacted to Mrs. Cazett's committee?

STUDENT REACTION SHEET

INSTRUCTOR _____ STUDENT _____

COURSE _____ DATE _____

CRITICAL INCIDENT _____

REACTION:

REFERENCES CITED

1. _____
2. _____
3. _____
4. _____

Support Services

SELECTED REFERENCES
SUPPORT SERVICES

Baker, Joseph J. and Jon S. Peters. *School Maintenance and Operation,* Danville, Ill.: Interstate Printers and Publishers, 1963.

Car, D. S. "Day the Janitor Was Sick," *Education Digest,* January 1972.

Castetter, Wm. B. *Administering the School Personnel Program,* New York: The Macmillen Company, 1962.

Fox, Willard and Alfred Schwartz. *Managerial Guide for School Principals,* Columbus, Ohio: Charles E. Merrill Books, Inc., 1965.

Jones, Florence G. *How to Run a More Effective School Office,* Englewood Cliffs, N.J.: Prentice-Hall, Inc., 1966.

"Maintenance Management: You Can't Overplan," *Nation's Schools,* Number 91, May 1973.

Maynard, R. "School Secretaries," *Business Education Forum,* Number 28, October 1973.

Mayshark, Cyprus. *Administration of School Health Programs: Its Theory and Practice,* St. Louis, Missouri: C. V. Mosley Co., 1967.

NEA Research Division. "Helping Teachers With Teacher Aides," *NEA Research Bulletin,* Number 50, May 1972.

Nugent, F. A. "School Counselors, Psychologists, and Social Workers: A Distinction," *Psychology in the Schools,* Number 10, July 1973.

Palette, N. "Defining the Role of the School Librarian," *School and Community.* Number 58, March 1972.

Parker, N. "School Nurse," *Today's Education,* Number 63, November 1974.

Reynolds, H. and M. E. Tramel. "Your Secretary," *School Management,* Number 15, July 1971.

Robinson, D. W. "Police in the Schools," *Today's Education,* Number 59, October 1970.

"Transportation: Problems and Prospects for 1973," *School Management,* Number 16, November 1972.

Chapter 9

Legal Problems

In modern day school management, questions about law constantly increase. Administrators go to court for innumerable causes and are ever in need to keep abreast with legal developments based on recent court decisions and new interpretations of the law. Due process, administrator liability, student rights, and the reasonable use of corporal punishment head the list of legal pressures confronting the educational manager.

This chapter presents critical incidents regarding conflict situations confronting educators in the area of law. It should be apparent to the professional educator that the number of law suits are on the increase. It is hoped that the questions posed and the material presented will enable the reader to develop a better understanding and appreciation for the problems confronting the modern day school manager.

The Great Imposter

Walkerville High School advertised for a district vocational director. Although the job description did not require a degree in educational administration, a degree would mean a salary of $26,000 instead of $21,000.

Jack Rossman applied for the job. As a result of his outstanding personality, he was awarded the position. Lacking a degree in educational administration, he assured the superintendent that during the summer months he would complete the degree. His college transcript listed enough college credits to qualify him for the position of vocational director.

Quite by accident, someone in Jack's office looked at his teaching certificate.

Legal Problems

For three years, he performed satisfactorily in that capacity. He completed his administrative degree and was awarded the higher salary as indicated in the job description. Jack's performance and especially his school loyalty pleased the superintendent.

It so happened that the teachers in the district were upset by several superintendent decisions. A rift developed between the education association and the central office. The teachers union initiated a financial investigation including expenditures and the district's accounting system. Jack Rossman, the vocational director, was within the scope of the investigation.

Quite by accident, someone in Jack's office looked at his teaching certificate displayed on the wall. Discrepancies in numbering and typing variations led to a check at the office of the State Department of Education. Word was phoned back that Jack's teaching certificate had not been issued, nor did the colleges listed on a transcript have records of credits as listed on his original application.

The State Department of Education was embarrassed by the loose record-keeping. At the same time, the superintendent defended Jack because of his job performance. The only group upset by Jack's action was the teachers union which demanded action.

DISCUSSION QUESTIONS

1. What action would you take to resolve the discrepancy in certification?
2. Legally could the board of education dismiss Mr. Rossman?
3. Identify the due process rights of the vocational director.
4. Should the job description be re-written to qualify Mr. Rossman for the position?
5. What type of job application procedures would have eliminated this problem?

Love is a Many Tenured Thing

Judy Splat, in her second year, was a beginning teacher at Cullman High School. She had not received tenure but would qualify at the beginning of her third year.

Bob Barker also taught at the high school. He had received tenure and was active in defending personal and professional rights of teachers. Both Judy and Bob were highly individualistic teachers who now and then found themselves placed against the rest of the staff members who were quite traditional.

As time passed, they were driven closer and closer together. They spent all of their breaks and preparation time together. One day Judy divorced her husband, and Bob's wife, seeking a legal separation, moved out of the house. Bob and Judy were so attached to each other, they held hands and often whispered to each other when other staff members neared them. At times they just stood silent and observed the students.

Because Cullman was a small community, board of education members soon understood how things were between the two teachers. Thereupon, the board president asked Mr. Paperwell, the principal, to end this school attachment between Bob and Judy. So Mr. Paperwell requested the couple to meet in his office for a conference.

At the beginning, Bob and Judy expressed the belief that they were being picked on because of their individualism in teaching. They contended that what they did with their lives was their own business.

They also asserted their belief in openness. Anything less would be a cop-out to themselves and their students. The teachers then threatened legal action if administrative harassment continued.

After the board meeting, the couple continued much as before, and citizens in the community kept pressuring the board of education and the high school principal.

DISCUSSION QUESTIONS

1. Do you feel the teachers have grounds for legal action against the board of education?
2. In your opinion, are the teachers conducting themselves in a professional manner?
3. What rights do teachers have to lead their own lives?
4. Can a board of education set standards for moral conduct among staff members?
5. What legal recourse does the principal have in resolving the above critical incident?

Legal Problems

The Birds and Bees

Ms. Genshaw had taught biology at Blakely High School for six years. She was held in great esteem for her professional conduct in the classroom and state and national organizations had cited her as an outstanding educator.

All tenth grade pupils were required to take her biology classes. Year after year, she included instruction dealing with sex education.

Barry Bushmit, one of her best pupils, was the son of the board president. At the dinner table one evening, Barry told his parents about a discussion of sex in Ms. Genshaw's class.

Barry's parents were incensed at sex education being taught in school. In addition, since Ms. Genshaw was single, perhaps her knowledge about sex education was strictly academic — the birds and bees stuff.

The next morning Mr. Bushmit telephoned the principal. He ordered the administrator to stop Ms. Genshaw's teaching sex education in biology or transfer Barry to another class. Mr. Bushmit demanded immediate action.

DISCUSSION QUESTIONS

1. Does a parent have the legal right to request or demand that their child be transferred to another class because of a disagreement with the teaching content of the class?
2. Does Ms. Genshaw have a legal right to teach sex education in her biology class?
3. What legal procedures should the board of education adopt to protect the academic freedom of a teacher?
4. What action would you take as principal regarding the request from the president of the board of education?
5. Do you feel that sex education should be taught in senior high schools? Explain your answer.

Confidential Information

"Mr. Jackson, I want to ask a favor of you." Shy Betty Hietman was making the request in the first period social studies class.

Critical Incidents In School Administration

"I'll be glad to do anything I can to help," responded Mr. Jackson.

"Could you excuse me from class and not mark me absent?"

"I should know why, don't you think, Betty?"

"I have a doctor's appointment, and I don't want my parents to know about it. If you mark me absent, the office will call my home and then they'd know," replied Betty.

"Is the doctor's appointment for what I think it is?" asked Mr. Jackson.

"Yes, I'm afraid so," was Betty's coy reply.

The next day in class Mr. Jackson proceeded as usual, but when the class ended, he stopped Betty.

"How's it going, Betty?"

She shook her head dejectedly. Tears filled her eyes.

"Want to talk about it?" asked Mr. Jackson. She did. She was pregnant.

Mr. Jackson explained options, but she was more concerned that her parents not know. She definitely did not want to get married. What she wanted was an abortion. Mr. Jackson, however, recommended she tell her parents. He also suggested the name of a clergyman who he knew counseled teenagers who faced abortion problems.

DISCUSSION QUESTIONS

1. What legal liability does Mr. Jackson have toward Betty and her parents?
2. Do the parents of Betty have legal recourse against the teacher for his discussion of the possibility of an abortion?
3. Should the principal formally reprimand Mr. Jackson for not following attendance policy in allowing Betty to miss class without marking her absent?
4. What action would you take regarding a pregnant girl that informed you she did not want to tell her parents about her pregnancy?
5. What role should the board of education play in establishing policy for the treatment of confidential information?

Legal Problems

Who's the Head Coach

Phil Kojak's varsity career as coach at Kindel High School had been a five-year tenure. His teams had won the state championship for the past two years, and once Phil had been named "Coach of the Year." Presently, because of a 6'11" center named Boots Builtwell, the team was undefeated.

Kindel was scheduled to play Inner City High School for the league championship. The winners would advance to the district tournament. The Inner City High's only defeat had occurred at the hands of Kindel. The stage was set for a showdown.

Al Durnbull had been the principal at Kindel High School for the past fifteen years. In his apprenticeship, he had served two years as assistant principal. Al was an egotist. He considered himself the best principal in the state. But he had a problem. He needed a "daily evening drink" which became a few too many. On the night of the Kindel-Inner City game, Al had a couple of drinks and reached the game "feeling no pain."

Fortunately Al was quiet during most of the four quarters. Then with three seconds remaining on the clock and the score knotted at 91, Phil Kojak called time-out. He planned to throw the ball from out-of-bounds toward the basket where Boots Builtwell would be ready and waiting.

The play worked perfectly. Only the Inner City guard very clearly fouled Boots, who unfortunately missed the shot. Time ran out, and no foul was called. Phil Kojak spoke heatedly to the official about the obvious foul. It did no good. The game would go into overtime — an additional three minutes.

While Phil told his players their assignments before the overtime period began, Al Durnbull, slightly dizzy, felt that as principal he could speak to the official.

"Didn't you see that foul?," Al shouted. He reeked of bourbon.

The official winced. "Look, Mr. Durnbull, go back to your seat and sit down."

"Don't tell me what to do. I'm the school principal. Just keep that in mind."

The official blew his whistle. It meant a technical against Kindel High School. Inner City caged the free throw and took possession of the ball. Ultimately, Inner City scored three points and won by one point.

As Al, now sobered up, approached the coach to apologize, Phil stormed away saying he would take the principal to court for his actions.

DISCUSSION QUESTIONS

1. Can a principal be sued by a teacher for unprofessional conduct?
2. Was the principal correct in protesting the decision of the official?
3. What legal action could the board of education take against the principal? The coach?
4. Has the principal violated any law by his attendance at the basketball game while under the influence of alcohol?
5. What procedures would you suggest to avoid future problems of administrator involvement with officials at athletic contests?

The Blonde Bomb

After Bill Bower's third day of student teaching at Willowside High, Nancy Johnson, an attractive blonde senior, asked if she could see him after class.

Nancy had big warm eyes and rolled them freely at Bill who had not discouraged her. She was a cute trick. The supervising teacher had discussed the problem of dating high school students only briefly; so Bill saw nothing wrong with talking to Nancy and smiling at her.

As she walked into the room at the end of the day, Nancy had all the poise and charm of a model. She was tall, sensuous, and well developed. Nancy wore a mini-skirt and a clinging sweater. Bill felt a bit shook by her appearance as she neared him. She opened her Shakespeare book and pointed to a passage in *Romeo and Juliet*. As she did this, she brushed her body against Bill's arm. He blushed but he dared not move. She might notice. At last, Nancy retreated a bit, and they continued the discussion. Finally, Nancy left the room.

That evening Bill felt the walls of his small apartment closing in on him. He decided to go for a walk. All of a sudden, a car was at curbside. He looked up. It was Nancy. "You want a ride, Mr. Bower?"

Now, he had been thinking of her all evening. He leaped at the chance to see her again. When they stopped at his apartment, Bill said "good night" and "thanks for the ride."

"Hey, man, aren't you going to ask me in?" She was pouting.

"O.K., O.K. Only for a minute." said Bill.

Legal Problems

When Bill closed the apartment door, Nancy threw her arms around his neck and kissed his mouth sensually. He pushed her away. But she exclaimed with a kiss, "If you don't make love to me, I'll scream rape." Bill tried to reason with her but to no avail. At last, he took her by the elbow and led her to her car. But he promised to see her on the weekend.

At the very instant they emerged from the apartment, Mr. Treadmore, Bill's supervising teacher, drove past. He waved as he passed them. Next morning at school, a note from the principal requested his presence at once! Bill paused to consider his position.

DISCUSSION QUESTIONS

1. Does the law say anything about teachers dating high school students? Explain your answer.
2. Explain a procedure that Bill might have used to discourage the actions of Nancy.
3. Are student teachers entitled to the same rights as regular staff members?
4. What action should Bill take if Nancy informed the principal that she had been raped by Mr. Bower?
5. What role should the administration play in orienting student teachers to the school setting?

Here Comes The Judge

Jack Harper was the principal of Potterville High School, a fashionable school in an affluent suburb. As the high school principal for seven years, he was highly respected for his liberal views and innovative educational practices.

Bill Ringstone, the son of a wealthy physician in the community, was a constant problem to Mr. Harper. The student had been suspended a number of times for petty rule violations. At the moment, he faced expulsion.

Bill was charged with "encouraging and participating in petty gambling, promoting disrespect for the faculty and staff, providing questionable weekend parties, and spreading malicious rumors." Dr. Ringstone was furious about his son's possible expulsion, and he threatened to take legal action on the grounds that the boy was entitled to the right to attend the public high school.

Critical Incidents In School Administration

The principal argued that his own duty was to protect the moral well-being of all the other students.

A meeting was scheduled involving the student, his father, and the principal.

Jack Harper spent a long time wondering exactly what to say at the conference.

DISCUSSION QUESTIONS

1. Do you feel students should be expelled from school so the moral well-being of other young people can be protected?
2. What position should Dr. Ringstone take to get his son re-admitted to Potterville High School?
3. Identify the legal rights of Bill Ringstone.
4. Should the board of education support the recommendation of the high school principal?
5. Is expulsion a defensible mechanism to control deviant behavior among high school students?

Superintendent Sues

The superintendent of schools in Middleville sued for $30,000 damages against leaders of a committee involved in a school board recall movement. He charged the group with defamation of character.

Don Woolside, the superintendent, said in the suit, filed in Monroe County Circuit Court, that statements made about him on petitions for an election to recall six of the seven board members, were untrue, libelous, and slanderous.

One accusation against the board members was their retention of Mr. Woolside as superintendent when he had not established himself as an educational leader. Another charge was that the board had failed to reprimand Mr. Woolside for holding a conference with teachers at a time when pupils should have had instruction in class.

Mr. Woolside denied the indictment and reasoned the charges had done harm to his reputation in the field of school administration. He asked the court to enjoin publication and circulation of the petitions.

Even though one of the board members who had been a recall target had resigned, the committee of critics still had petitions circulating against the five other board members. All petitions contained what Mr. Woolside said were libelous and slanderous statements.

DISCUSSION QUESTIONS

1. Can a superintendent of schools sue a recall petition committee?
2. What legal action could the board of education members take regarding activities of the petition recall committee?
3. What are the legal implications of the wording on the recall petitions?
4. What recommendations can you give to Superintendent Woolside?
5. Explain the legal implications of recalling the board of education members that have been elected.

A River Happening

Each year among the varied senior class activities at Baxter High, the seniors planned an annual canoe trip. It was always scheduled during the week of "senior skip week." Although seniors were not required to participate, many chose to go along. The seniors were required to follow the same school policies that applied to other school-sponsored activites. The class treasury subsidized the floating event, but the board covered the cost of transportation.

As a rule, normal attendance was approximately 75, about one-half of the class. Chaperones were chosen from those who had experience in canoeing, water safety instructor training, and first aid. Usually, administrators, teachers, and parents accompanied the canoeists.

The annual trip went well until near the end. Then a seventeen year old girl was rammed by a canoe. When the sponsors arrived, she was lying on the riverbank. She was in a great deal of pain and clearly was suffering from shock. An ambulance carried her to the hospital.

As a minor (17) she could not be treated without parental consent. All attempts to reach her parents by telephone failed.

DISCUSSION QUESTIONS

1. Can the class sponsors legally give their consent for treatment?
2. What liability does the school have in accidents resulting from a school-sponsored activity?
3. Could the principal be sued for negligence because of the injury to the girl?
4. What procedures would you take to avoid legal liability suits on school-sponsored field trips?
5. Should treatment be administered to an injured student without parental consent? Explain your answer.

SELECTED REFERENCES
LEGAL PROBLEMS

Johnson, George Marion. *Handbook on Michigan Education Law,* East Lansing, Mi.: Michigan State University Press, 1970.

Kern, A., Ray Corns and Walter McCann. *1973 Supplement to Public School Law,* St. Paul, Minn.: West Publishing Co., 1973.

Morris, Arval A. *The Constitution and American Education,* St. Paul, Minn.: West Publishing Company, 1974.

NOLPE, *Current Trends in School Law,* Topeka, Ka: The National Organization on Legal Problems of Education, 1974.

NOLPE, *Frontiers of School Law,* Topeka, Ka: The National Organization on Legal Problems of Education, 1972,

STUDENT REACTION SHEET

INSTRUCTOR _____   STUDENT _____

COURSE _____   DATE _____

CRITICAL INCIDENT _____

REACTION:

_____

_____

_____

_____

_____

_____

_____

_____

_____

_____

_____

_____

_____

_____

_____

_____

_____

REFERENCES CITED

1. _____
2. _____
3. _____
4. _____